# contents

# a c k n o w l e d g e m e n t s

The author would like to thank the following people who have been instrumental in the preparation of this book: Mike Gilbert, Rosemarie Griffiths, Hedgehog Design, Richard Holt, Barbara Jones, Jon Moore, and Roger Petheram.

Osborne Books is grateful to the following for giving permission for the reproduction of original material: Department of Trade and Industry, Sage Plc and Tesco Plc. Thanks are also due to QCA and the Awarding Bodies for their invaluable help and advice during the preparation of the text.

# a u t h o r

Michael Fardon has worked in international banking and lectured in banking and finance before becoming Managing Editor at Osborne Books. He has written and co-authored a number of financial, business education and Key Skills books and resource packs. He has also been involved in the drafting and editing of GNVQ qualifications for QCA and Edexcel.

# teaching notes

### the text

Advanced Finance covers the Business Finance Unit and the financial content of the Business Planning Unit of the Advanced Vocational Certificate of Education in Business. The content has been taken from the best-selling Advanced Business from Osborne Books.

### tutor pack

A Tutor Pack is available for this book. It contains answers to the Activities, and two sample external test papers and photocopiable material. If you would like to find out more about this Pack, please contact the Osborne Books Sales Office on 01905 748071.

### internal assessment and student activities

It is recommended that students should compile a Portfolio for AVCE Units, including those that are externally assessed, such as the Business Finance Unit. The planning of the chapters and Activities in this book have therefore been based very much around the assessment grids published by the Awarding Bodies.

### feedback

Osborne Books welcomes your feedback on this book. We appreciate both positive and negative comments which originate from teachers and from students. Please let us know by mail, e-mail (books@osbornebooks.co.uk) and telephone (01905 748071) and we will take note of everything you have to say, and will respond.

Michael Fardon, Spring 2001.

# s t u d e n t  n o t e s

## what is a Vocational course?

The word 'Vocational' means that the qualification relates to an area of work – in your case the business world. In the course that you will be doing you will be given the knowledge and skills you will need in a variety of business careers. The qualification means being able to 'do' a job as well as 'knowing' about it. It provides skills that employers value. Your qualification will also enable you to progress to higher education, which in turn will open up many possibilities for careers in business.

## what is a Unit?

Units are areas of study which make up the course. Some are compulsory, some are optional. This book contains the financial content of two Units:

**Business finance**
Finance is essential to all businesses. This Unit investigates the way in which businesses manage their finances and shows how financial information can be interpreted to provide a picture of their financial 'health'.

**Business planning**
This Unit takes a practical look at the way in which a business plan is drawn up, incorporating a sales and marketing plan, a production and resources plan and a financial plan.

## Unit portfolios

Two thirds of the Units you cover are assessed through your coursework which is presented in a Portfolio – a folder containing your work which is known as Assessment Evidence. This is the work you have collected together so that you can be graded by your Assessor. The grades you can get range from A to E. Although the assessment for the Business Finance Unit is by external test, you are recommended to compile a Portfolio for this Unit to help you with revision.

## Unit external tests

One third of the Units you cover are assessed by an External Test set by your Awarding Body. There is a separate test for each unit. If you are doing the twelve Unit award, these Units are 'The Competitive Business Environment' and 'Business Finance'.

These tests are likely to contain a combination of short answer questions and Case Study work. You will be given plenty of practice in doing these tests.

## how the chapters are organised

The chapters in this book begin with an introduction which tells you what the chapter is about and what you will learn from it.

The chapters finish with a summary and key terms telling you what you should have learnt. Do not skip these sections – they are there to help you. The chapters also contain Activities for classwork and for investigation. These are Activities which will help build up Assessment Evidence for your Portfolio or give you practice for the external tests.

## information – the internet

One of the best and most comprehensive sources of up-to-date business information is the internet. The problem is really that there is almost too much information available. You need to be selective in what you find and print out.

You can access business websites direct, or can do a search on a particular word, for example 'co-operative' to find out about specific types of business. A good search engine can be found on www.yahoo.co.uk

As a start, for a useful and informative site which contains a wealth of information about a wide range of businesses, try Biz/ed, the educational website:

www.bized.ac.uk

Try the following for business finance and planning:

www.barclays.co.uk              www.hsbc.co.uk

www.dti.gov.uk                  www.hm-treasury.gov.uk

Lastly, if you need blank financial documents for the 'Business Finance' Unit, access our website, download the file from the resources section and then print out your documents. The address is:

www.osbornebooks.co.uk

Surf creatively!

# Financial recording and financial documents

## introduction

Every business has its stakeholders – its owners, its employees, customers, suppliers, lenders and other people and bodies who have an interest in what the business is doing. Stakeholders will want to know about the financial state of the business – whether the business is making a profit, can pay its wages, settle its bills, whether it is worth investing in. A business therefore needs to keep accurate financial records so that it can supply reliable information to these stakeholders.

In this chapter we take an overview of the way a business organises and uses financial information. We also look in detail at financial documents and see how they are completed and used to carry out financial transactions.

## what you will learn from this chapter

● the stakeholders of a business between them need to know about the sales, profit and value of a business

● this financial information is available in the financial statements of a business, which are taken from the business accounting system; it is essential that this information is accurate

● the starting point of the accounting system of a business is the documentation generated by financial transactions

● when a business buys or sells goods and services a number of documents 'flow' between the buyer and seller; these can vary depending on whether the payment is to be made straightaway or later (on credit)

● when a business deals with these financial documents it is essential that it is accurate and that it checks them carefully

# the need for financial recording

If anyone asks you how much you yourself are worth at any particular time, or how much you have spent within a particular period, you will probably be unable to give an accurate figure because you are unlikely to have kept a full record of every financial transaction you have carried out.

A business, on the other hand, must keep books to record its financial transactions. It will carry out the process of financial record keeping to provide information for a number of interested parties – its stakeholders. Look at the diagram below and read the text carefully . . .

| STAKEHOLDERS | WHAT ARE THEY INTERESTED IN? | WHY ARE THEY INTERESTED? |
|---|---|---|
| Owners/shareholders/managers | • Has the business made a profit?<br>• Can the business pay its way?<br>• Are the sales figures increasing? | • To see how much profit can be paid by the business to the owners/shareholders.<br>• To assess if the business will continue in the foreseeable future.<br>• To see if the business is growing. |
| Inland Revenue | • Has the business made a profit? | • To calculate the tax due on profit. |
| H M Customs and Excise | • What were the figures for sales and VAT charged on sales? | • To ensure that VAT charged on products is paid to H M Customs and Excise. |
| Bank manager/lender | • Has the business made a profit?<br>• What is the bank balance or overdraft?<br>• What is the value of the business? | • To check if the business can afford to make loan repayments.<br>• To decide how much the bank can lend to the business. |
| Employees and trade unions | • Has the business made a profit?<br>• Can the business continue to pay its way? | • To see if the business can afford pay rises.<br>• To assess if the business will continue to provide jobs in the foreseeable future. |
| Customers | • Is the business reliable and will it continue to trade? | • To see if the business has the financial stability to carry out work for its customers. |
| Suppliers (people to whom the business owes money) | • Is the business trading profitably?<br>• Are the bills being paid on time? | • To assess if the business is able to pay its bills on the due date. |
| Competitors | • What are the sales figures? | • To see if the business is expanding or declining and to consider whether the business is worth taking over. |

## the stakeholders

The stakeholders are:

- people inside the business – the owners, employees and managers
- people the business deals with – its customers and suppliers
- people who want to invest in the business or lend money to it
- bodies that want to tax the business – the Inland Revenue (taxation of profits) and H M Customs & Excise (collecting VAT charged on products)

The diagram on the previous page shows that different stakeholders need to know different types of financial information, including:

- sales figures and profit
- the value of the business

These figures are available in the 'financial statements' of the business.

When you have finished studying this unit you will see that the financial statements ('final accounts') are drawn up as the last part of a process in which data from financial documents is entered in the 'books' of the business, which in turn are used to provide figures for the final accounts. These then provide the information needed by the stakeholders.

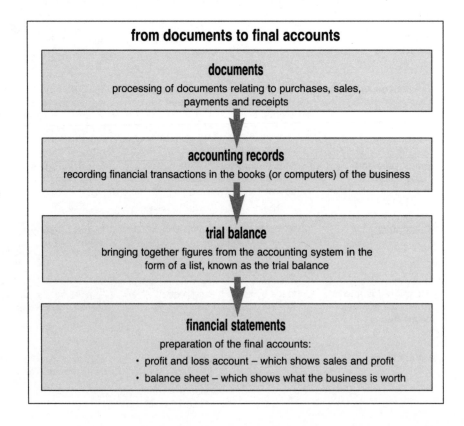

**from documents to final accounts**

**documents**
processing of documents relating to purchases, sales, payments and receipts

**accounting records**
recording financial transactions in the books (or computers) of the business

**trial balance**
bringing together figures from the accounting system in the form of a list, known as the trial balance

**financial statements**
preparation of the final accounts:
- profit and loss account – which shows sales and profit
- balance sheet – which shows what the business is worth

### the need for accurate financial records

It may sound like stating the obvious to say that financial records must be accurate, but a business which does not have accurate financial records may run into serious problems.

Think about the following examples . . .

- a business that makes mistakes loses the confidence of its customers
- a business that overcharges loses its customers
- a business that overstates its sales figures overstates its profit and pays too much tax
- a business that overstates its sales figures and overstates its profit gives a false impression of its performance to its owners and shareholders
- a business that understates its sales figures understates its profit and pays too little tax
- a business that pays too little tax can get into trouble with the Inland Revenue
- a business that understates its sales figures and its profit can lose the confidence of its managers, shareholders and lenders.

You should be able to think of other examples.

## Activity 1.1

# Stakeholders and financial records

1   Identify four different stakeholders of a business and state why each of the stakeholders will be interested in what the financial records of the business have to say about the financial 'health' of the business. Try to supplement what it says in textbooks with information you can gather from people working in business and dealing with businesses on a day-to-day basis.

2   State why you think it is important that the financial records of a business are accurate.

What are the implications of the following problems, all caused by inaccurate record keeping?

(a) A business receives a part payment of £1,000 from its customer in settlement of debts totalling £10,000 but records it in its books as a payment for £10,000?

(b) Somebody thinking of investing in a company is told that the profit figure is £65,000 when in fact it is £95,000?

(c) The Inland Revenue discovers that the business in (b) has underestimated its profit figure by £30,000?

## financial documents

In the next few chapters we will be dealing in a practical way with the processing of the figures through the accounting system of a business and the production of the final accounts – the profit and loss statement and the balance sheet.

In this chapter, however, we will concentrate on the first stage in the accounting process – the completion and use of financial documents. As we will see, different types of document are used in different types of transaction. The main distinction to be drawn is between cash transactions and credit transactions.

### cash transactions and credit transactions

When a business sells goods or services it will either ask for payment to be made straightaway or at a later date:

- a *cash sale* is when payment is made straightaway, for example when you buy goods in a shop
- a *credit sale* is when payment is made at a later date, for example when a business orders supplies and pays later 'on account'

The words 'cash sale' used in this way do not mean that just cash (in the form of notes and coins) is used – a 'cash sale' can be made using cash or a cheque. 'Cash' here means 'on the nail', ie immediate payment.

### documents used in cash transactions

Take for example an employee of a business going out into the town and buying some coloured photocopying paper needed urgently in the office or paying an engineer for repairs carried out. The transaction is very simple: payment is made by cash or cheque and a receipt is issued by the seller.

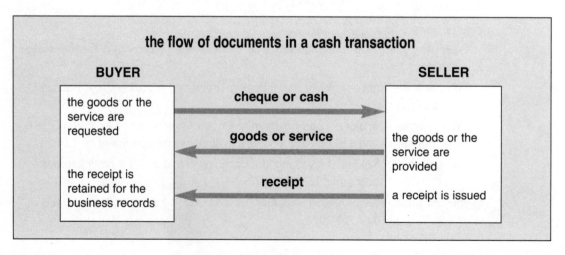

**the flow of documents in a cash transaction**

BUYER                                                    SELLER

| the goods or the service are requested | **cheque or cash** → | |
| | ← **goods or service** | the goods or the service are provided |
| the receipt is retained for the business records | ← **receipt** | a receipt is issued |

## till receipt

When someone makes a cash purchase for a business – for example going out to buy some stationery – it is important that they obtain a receipt because the business needs to record the fact that money has been spent on stationery – it is a running expense of the business

When the purchase is made cash tills show on the screen the money amount of the purchase and also the change to be given. The till will also issue a receipt for all purchases when cash, a cheque, a debit card or a credit card is used. In the example below a customer has bought a pack of coloured paper and some disks from Everest Stationery. A till receipt has been issued.

| | | |
|---|---|---|
| **Everest Stationery** | | retailer |
| **15 High St Mereford** | | address |
| **08 10 00  15.07** | | date and time of transaction |
| **Salesperson Tina** | | salesperson |
| **A4 paper (blue)** | **5.99** | goods purchased |
| **Disks** | **8.99** | goods purchased |
| **TOTAL** | **14.98** | total due |
| **CASH** | **20.00** | £20 (probably a £20 note) given by the customer |
| **CHANGE** | **5.02** | change given |
| **Thank you for your custom** | | personal message to help public relations |
| **Please retain this receipt in case of any query** | | advice to retain receipt in case of a problem with the goods |
| **VAT REG 373 2888 11** | | VAT Registration number |

## written receipt

Some businesses will write out a receipt on request, particularly if VAT needs to be shown (see the next page for an explanation of this). The example below is for the supply of more photocopier paper.

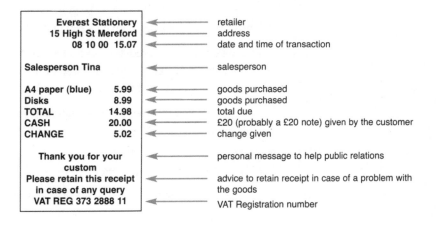

| Enigma Stationery | RECEIPT | No. 765 | receipt number |
|---|---|---|---|
| 14 High Street, Broadfield BR1 5FT | | | |
| VAT Reg 343 7645 23 | | | |
| Customer......... *H N Ford* ........................date...... *4 April 2000* ..... | | | customer name and date |
| *50 reams lasercopy paper (white) @ £4.00 each* | | *200.00* | description and price of goods |
| *50 reams lasercopy paper (blue) @ £4.00 each* | | *200.00* | |
| | | *400.00* | total of goods before VAT |
| | VAT | *70.00* | VAT charged |
| | TOTAL | *470.00* | total paid |

### some notes on Value Added Tax (VAT)

You will see that the till receipt shown on the previous page quotes a VAT (Value Added Tax) number but no VAT amount. Receipts and invoices for purchases under £100 do not have to show the VAT amount separately – it is included in the final amount. If you think about it, most till receipts you get from shops do not show the VAT amount, but you still pay it!

VAT is quoted on a number of the financial documents you will be studying and you will need to know what it is and how it works:

• VAT (Value Added Tax) is a government tax on the selling price charged for most goods and services.

• There are some exceptions – eg VAT is not charged on books or food.

• Most businesses with sales above a certain amount must register for VAT.

A business which is registered for VAT charges VAT at the standard rate (currently 17.5 per cent) on the money value of the goods or services it sells. The formula for working out the VAT charged on a sale is:

$$\text{VAT charged} = \text{Sales amount} \times \frac{17.5}{100}$$

For example, if the business sells goods or services for £200 it has to add on 17.5% of the £200 to the amount charged, ie

$$\text{VAT} = £200 \times \frac{17.5}{100} = £35.00$$

The total amount the business receives will be:

$$£200 \text{ plus } £35.00 \text{ (VAT)} = £235.00$$

The business will keep the £200 but will have to pay the £35 to HM Customs & Excise, the government department which administers VAT.

## Activity 1.2

# Completing receipts

You work in 'Helios' – a lighting shop. During the course of a day you write out three receipts to customers:

1  2 flexilamps @ £13.99, plus 2 candlelight bulbs @85p each sold to George Meredith.

2  1 standard lamp @ £149.95, plus one 100 watt bulb @ 99p, sold to  Alex Bell.

3  2 Georgian lamps @ £35.99 sold to Miss S Fox.

What will you charge each customer? You will add VAT to all three purchases and use the current rate of VAT. If you can, complete three blank receipts with the details.

## the cheque

Cheques are provided by the banks for their customers so that they can pay people specific sums of money. Cheques are used both for cash transactions and also for settling accounts for credit transactions (where payment is made later). The cheque shown below is the cheque used for the cash sale which produced the receipt at the bottom of page 13. Cheques are normally provided by the banks for their customers in books with counterfoils. When the cheque is written out the details (amount, date and person being paid) are recorded on the counterfoil and the cheque is torn out and given or posted to the person being paid. See pages 27 and 28 for more on cheques.

tear off
cheque
here

Date 4/4/00

Pay
*Enigma
Stationery*

£ 470.00

083772

counterfoil

**Albion Bank PLC**

7 The Avenue
Broadfield BR1 2AJ

Date    *4 April 2000*    90 47 17

Pay  *Enigma Stationery*

*Four hundred and seventy pounds only*   A/c payee only   £ 470.00 —

HARRIS N FORD

*Harris N Ford*

083772    90 47 17    11719881

cheque

## what happens to the cheque?

The cheque shown above is paid into the bank account of Enigma Stationery on a paying-in slip (see page 29) and will be cleared through the bank clearing system to Harris N Ford's bank. The cheque will then appear on Harris N Ford's bank statement (see page 31 for an example) as a deduction of £470 from the bank account. This process is shown in the diagram below.

Harris N Ford writes out a cheque for £470, dates it and signs it

▼

the cheque is given to Enigma Stationery for the paper supplied

▼

the cheque is paid in on a paying-in slip at Enigma Stationery's bank

▼

£470 will be added to the bank account of Enigma Stationery

▼

the cheque will be sent through a bank clearing system to Harris N Ford's bank – Albion Bank – and the £470 will be deducted from his account – and show on his bank statement

## making a purchase on credit

### financial documents for transaction 'on credit'

When a business buys goods or services *on credit* it orders the goods first and then pays later. During this process a number of different financial documents will be issued by the seller and the buyer. We will look in this chapter at a whole range of financial documents by means of a Case Study involving the purchase of fashion clothes.

You must bear in mind that not all purchases involve all the documents listed below. Many purchases are for services, eg office cleaning, and do not involve goods being sent. It is important for your studies, however, that

• you can recognise each of the documents

• you know what they are for

• you can complete a number of them

The financial documents shown here include:

– **purchase order**, which the buyer sends to the seller

– **delivery note**, which goes with the goods from the seller to the buyer

– **goods received note**, which is sometimes completed by the buyer to record the actual amount of goods received

– **invoice**, which lists the goods and tells the buyer what is owed

– **credit note**, which is sent to the buyer if any refund is due

– **statement of account**, sent by the seller to remind the buyer what is owed

– **remittance advice**, sent by the buyer when the goods are paid for

– **cheque**, which is completed by the buyer to pay for the goods

– **paying-in slip**, used for paying a cheque into a bank account

– **bank statement**, which records payments in and out of the bank account

### the flow of documents

Before you read the Case Study, examine the diagram set out on the next page. Down the columns representing the buyer and the seller are various activities which lead to transactions, which in turn generate documents.

As we have just seen, you should appreciate that not all the activities happen all the time. Mostly, however, things run smoothly and the invoice is paid following receipt of a statement of account.

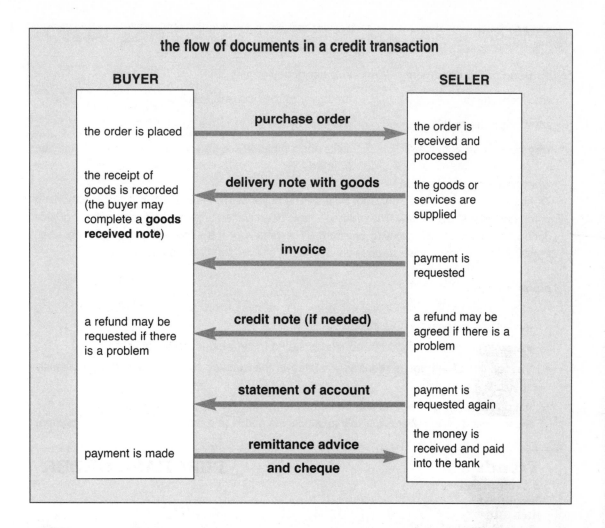

## the flow of documents in a credit transaction

| BUYER | | SELLER |
|---|---|---|
| the order is placed | **purchase order** → | the order is received and processed |
| the receipt of goods is recorded (the buyer may complete a **goods received note**) | ← **delivery note with goods** | the goods or services are supplied |
| | ← **invoice** | payment is requested |
| a refund may be requested if there is a problem | ← **credit note (if needed)** | a refund may be agreed if there is a problem |
| | ← **statement of account** | payment is requested again |
| payment is made | **remittance advice and cheque** → | the money is received and paid into the bank |

## Case Study

# Cool Socks
## buying on credit

Cool Socks Limited manufactures fashion socks in a variety of colours. It supplies a number of different customers, including Trends, a fashion store in Broadfield.

In this Case Study we see an order for 100 pairs of socks placed by Trends with Cool Socks. The socks are delivered, but some are found to be faulty, so a refund has to be made. Finally, payment has to be made for the socks.

The Case Study looks in detail at the purchase and sales documents involved. Now read on.

## PURCHASE ORDER – the buyer orders the goods

| | |
|---|---|
| **purpose of the document** | to order goods or services |
| **who completes it?** | the buyer of the goods or services |
| **what happens to it?** | it is sent by the buyer to the seller |
| **why must it be accurate?** | if it is not completed accurately the wrong products may be ordered |

**what happens in this case?**

Trends orders some socks from Cool Socks. The buyer at Trends will post or fax the authorised purchase order shown below. The order will have been written or printed out in the office, or produced on a computer accounting program. The details of the socks will have been obtained from Cool Socks' catalogue, or possibly by means of a written or telephoned enquiry.

**points to note:**

• each purchase order has a specific reference number – this is useful for filing and quoting on later documents such as invoices and statements

• the product code of the goods required is stated in the product code column

• the quantity of the goods required is stated in the quantity column – socks are obviously supplied in pairs!

• the purchase order is signed and dated by the person in charge of purchasing – without this authorisation the supplier is unlikely to supply the goods (the order will probably be returned)

---

# Trends          PURCHASE ORDER

**4 Friar Street**
**Broadfield**
**BR1 3RF**
Tel 01908 761234  Fax 01908 761987
VAT REG GB 0745 8383 56

| Cool Socks Limited, | purchase order no | 47609 |
|---|---|---|
| Unit 45 Elgar Estate, | date | 25 09 00 |
| Broadfield, | | |
| BR7 4ER | | |

| product code | quantity | description |
|---|---|---|
| 45B | 100 pairs | Blue Toebar socks |

**AUTHORISED**    signature..........*D Signer*.........................................................date....*25/09/00*........

---

see page 35 for an activity involving this document

## DELIVERY NOTE  – the goods are delivered

| | |
|---|---|
| **purpose of the document** | it states what goods are being delivered |
| **who completes it?** | the seller of the goods |
| **what happens to it?** | it is sent by the seller to the buyer |
| **why must it be accurate?** | if the goods delivered do not tally with the description on the delivery note, the goods may be refused |

**what happens in this case?**

The delivery note is despatched with the goods when the order is ready. It is normally printed out in the office, often by a computer accounting program. In this case, the delivery note travels with the socks, and a copy will be signed by Trends on receipt.

**points to note:**

- the delivery note has a numerical reference, useful for filing and later reference if there is a query
- the delivery note quotes the purchase order number – this enables the buyer to 'tie up' the delivery with the original order
- the details of the goods supplied – the quantity and the description – will be checked against the goods themselves
- the delivery note will be signed and dated by the person receiving the goods

---

### ── DELIVERY NOTE ──
# COOL SOCKS LIMITED

Unit 45 Elgar Estate, Broadfield, BR7 4ER
Tel 01908 765314  Fax 01908 765951
VAT REG GB 0745 4672 76

Trends
4 Friar Street
Broadfield
BR1 3RF

| | |
|---|---|
| delivery note no | 68873 |
| delivery method | Lynx Parcels |
| your order | 47609 |
| date | 02 10 00 |

| product code | quantity | description |
|---|---|---|
| 45B | 100 pairs | Blue Toebar socks |

**Received**

signature.....*V Williams*.....name (capitals)..*V WILLIAMS*.....date..*5/10/00*.....

**see page 35 for an activity involving this document**

## GOODS RECEIVED NOTE – the buyer records receipt of the goods

**purpose of the document**     it records what goods have been delivered

**who completes it?**     the buyer of the goods

**what happens to it?**     it is kept by the buyer

**why must it be accurate?**     a mistake may result in a problem with the delivery not being picked up

**what happens in this case?**

The goods received note (GRN) will be completed by the person in Trends who looks after the stock. In the case of this delivery, ten pairs of the socks have been received damaged – Trends will want a refund.

**points to note:**

- details of the goods are noted on the form
- the condition of the goods – the damage to the socks – is recorded and this fact will be notified on separate copies to the buyer, to Accounts and to the stockroom
- a goods received note is not used by all businesses

---

# Trends                    GOODS RECEIVED NOTE

**Supplier**

| Cool Socks Limited, Unit 45 Elgar Estate, Broadfield, BR7 4ER | GRN no | 1871 |
| | date | 05 10 00 |

| quantity | description | order number |
| --- | --- | --- |
| 100 pairs | Blue Toebar socks | 47609 |

**carrier**   Lynx Parcels          consignment no   8479347

**received by**   *V Williams*          checked by   *R Patel*

| condition of goods (please tick and comment) | good condition damaged ✓ (10 pairs) shortages | copies to Buyer ✓ Accounts ✓ Stockroom ✓ |

see page 38 for an activity involving this document

## INVOICE – payment is requested by the seller (see next page)

| | |
|---|---|
| **purpose of the document** | it tells the buyer how much is owed and when it has to be paid |
| **who completes it?** | the seller of the goods |
| **what happens to it?** | it is sent by the seller to the buyer, who checks it carefully and keeps it on file for reference |
| **why must it be accurate?** | a mistake could result in the wrong amount being paid |

**what happens in this case?**

The invoice, like the delivery note, is prepared in the seller's office, and is written out or produced on a computer accounting program. Invoices produced by different organisations will vary to some extent in terms of detail, but their basic layout will always be the same.

The invoice prepared by Cool Socks Ltd – illustrated on the next page – is typical of a modern computer-printed document.

**points to note**:

**addresses**

The invoice shows the address:

- of the seller/supplier of the goods – Cool Socks Limited
- the place where the invoice should be sent – to Trends
- where the goods are to be sent – it may not always be the same as the invoice address; for example a supermarket ordering a container load of bananas will ask them to be delivered to a distribution warehouse, not to the Accounts Department!

**references**

There are a number of important references on the invoice:

- the numerical reference of the invoice itself – 787923
- the account number allocated to Trends by the seller – 3993 – for use in the seller's and the purchaser's financial records for reference purposes
- the original reference number on the purchase order sent by Trends – 47609 – which will enable the shop to 'tie up' the invoice with the original order

Now look at the document and the explanations on the next two pages to find out what you have to check when you receive an invoice.

**see pages 35 to 37 for activities involving this document**

**INVOICE – payment is requested by the seller**

## INVOICE

# COOL SOCKS LIMITED

Unit 45 Elgar Estate, Broadfield, BR7 4ER
Tel 01908 765314  Fax 01908 765951
VAT REG GB 0745 4672 76

invoice to

Trends
4 Friar Street
Broadfield
BR1 3RF

| | |
|---|---|
| invoice no | 787923 |
| account | 3993 |
| your reference | 47609 |
| date/tax point | 02 10 00 |

| product code | description | quantity | price | unit | total | discount % | net |
|---|---|---|---|---|---|---|---|
| 45B | Blue Toebar socks | 100 | 2.36 | pair | 236.00 | 0.00 | 236.00 |

| | |
|---|---|
| GOODS TOTAL | 236.00 |
| VAT | 41.30 |
| TOTAL | 277.30 |

**terms**
30 days

# points to note and check on the invoice

You will need to check that the reference number quoted here ties up with your purchase order number.

The date here is normally the date on which the goods have been sent. It is known as the 'invoice date'. The date is important for calculating when the invoice is due to be paid. In this case the 'terms' (see the bottom left-hand corner of the invoice) are 30 days. This means the invoice is due to be paid within 30 days after the invoice date (2 October), so it is due to be paid by 31 October.

The arithmetic and details in this line must be checked very carefully to make sure that you pay  the correct amount for what you have ordered:

- product code – this is the catalogue number which appeared on the original purchase order and on the delivery note
- description – this must agree with the description on the purchase order
- quantity – this should agree with the quantity ordered
- price – this is the price of each unit shown in the next column
- unit is the way in which the unit is counted up and charged for, eg units (single items), pairs (as here), or 10s,100s and so on
- total is the unit price multiplied by the number of units
- discount % is the percentage allowance (known as trade discount) given to trusted customers who regularly deal with the supplier, ie they receive a certain percentage (eg 10%) deducted from their bill

  – note that cash discount is also sometimes allowed – this is a percentage (eg 2.5%) deducted from the net amount before VAT is added on
- net is the amount due to the seller after deduction of trade discount, and before VAT is added on

The Goods Total is the total of the column above it. It is the final amount due to the seller before VAT is added on.

Value Added Tax (VAT) is calculated and added on – here it is 17.5% of the Goods Total, ie £236.00 x 17.5%  =  £41.30. The VAT is then added to the Goods Total to produce the actual amount owing: £236.00  +  £41.30  =  £277.30
Note that if a cash discount is taken, the VAT is calculated on the Goods Total after the discount has been deducted.

The 'terms' explain the conditions on which the goods are supplied. '30 days' means that payment has to be made within 30 days of the invoice date. Any cash discount is also noted here, eg '2.5% for settlement within 7 days of invoice'

## CREDIT NOTE – the seller gives a refund

| | |
|---|---|
| **purpose of the document** | A credit note is a 'refund' document which reduces the amount owed by the buyer. The format of a credit note is very similar to that of an invoice. |
| **who completes it?** | the seller of the goods |
| **what happens to it?** | it is sent by the seller to the buyer, who checks it carefully and keeps it on file with the invoice |
| **why must it be accurate?** | a mistake could result in the wrong amount eventually being paid |

**what happens in this case?**

Trends has received 10 damaged pairs of socks. These will be sent back with a document known as a Returns Note to Cool Socks with a request for credit – ie a reduction in the bill for the 10 faulty pairs. Cool Socks will have to issue the credit note for £27.73 shown below.

**points to note:**

* a credit note can be issued for faulty goods, missing goods, or goods which are not needed
* the credit note quotes the invoice number and states why the credit (refund) is being given

——————— **CREDIT NOTE** ———————

# COOL SOCKS LIMITED

Unit 45 Elgar Estate, Broadfield, BR7 4ER
Tel 01908 765314  Fax 01908 765951
VAT REG GB 0745 4672 76

to

Trends
4 Friar Street
Broadfield
BR1 3RF

| | |
|---|---|
| credit note no | 12157 |
| account | 3993 |
| your reference | 47609 |
| our invoice | 787923 |
| date/tax point | 10 10 00 |

| product code | description | quantity | price | unit | total | discount % | net |
|---|---|---|---|---|---|---|---|
| 45B | Blue Toebar socks | 10 | 2.36 | pair | 23.60 | 0.00 | 23.60 |

**Reason for credit**
10 pairs of socks received damaged
(Your returns note no. R/N 2384)

| | |
|---|---|
| GOODS TOTAL | 23.60 |
| VAT | 4.13 |
| TOTAL | 27.73 |

**see pages 39 to 40 for activities involving this document**

## STATEMENT OF ACCOUNT – the seller requests payment

| **purpose of the document** | a statement of account – which is normally issued at the end of every month – tells the buyer how much is owed |
| **who completes it?** | the seller of the goods |
| **what happens to it?** | it is sent by the seller to the buyer who checks it against the invoices and credit notes on file |
| **why must it be accurate?** | a mistake could result in the wrong amount being paid |

**what happens in this case?**

A seller will not normally expect a buyer to pay each individual invoice as soon as it is received. Instead, a statement of account showing what is owed is sent by the seller to the buyer at the end of the month. It shows:

- invoices issued for goods supplied – the full amount due, including VAT
- refunds made on credit notes – including VAT
- payments received from the buyer (if any)

The statement issued by Cool Socks to Trends for the period covering the sale (the invoice) and refund (the credit note) is shown below. Trends now has to pay the £249.57 owing.

**STATEMENT OF ACCOUNT**

# COOL SOCKS LIMITED

Unit 45 Elgar Estate, Broadfield, BR7 4ER
Tel 01908 765314  Fax 01908 765951
VAT REG GB 0745 4672 76

TO

Trends
4 Friar Street
Broadfield
BR1 3RF

account    3993

date    31 10 00

| date | details | debit £ | credit £ | balance £ |
|---|---|---|---|---|
| 02 10 00 | Invoice 787923 | 277.30 | | 277.30 |
| 10 10 00 | Credit note 12157 | | 27.73 | 249.57 |
| | | | **AMOUNT NOW DUE** | 249.57 |

see pages 40 to 41 for activities involving this document

## REMITTANCE ADVICE – the buyer sends a payment advice

| | |
|---|---|
| **purpose of the document** | a remittance advice is a document sent by the buyer to the seller stating that payment is being made |
| **who completes it?** | the buyer |
| **what happens to it?** | it is sent by the buyer to the seller |
| **why must it be accurate?** | a mistake could result in the wrong amount being paid |

**what happens in this case?**

Trends have completed a remittance advice listing the invoice that is being paid and the credit note which is being deducted from the amount owing. Trends will make out a cheque for the total amount of the remittance advice. This is shown on the next page. It will be attached to the remittance advice and will be posted to Cool Socks in November.

**points to note:**

- the remittance advice quotes the account number (3993) allocated to Trends by Cool Socks – this will help Cool Socks to update their records when the payment is received
- the documents are listed in the columns provided: 'your reference' describes the documents issued by Cool Socks and quotes their numbers; 'our reference' quotes the number of the Purchase Order originally issued by Trends
- the amounts of the invoice and the credit note are entered in the right-hand column – note that the credit note amount is negative, so it is shown in brackets; the total payment amount is shown in the box at the bottom of the form – this will be the amount of the cheque issued
- payment can alternatively be made by computer transfer between bank accounts (BACS); in this case a remittance advice is still sent, but no cheque
- a 'tear-off' printed remittance advice listing all the items is sometimes attached to the statement sent by the seller; all the buyer has to do is to tick the items being paid, and pay!

TO         **REMITTANCE ADVICE**   FROM

Cool Socks Limited
Unit 45 Elgar Estate,
Broadfield, BR7 4ER

**Trends**
4 Friar Street
Broadfield
BR1 3RF
Tel 01908 761234  Fax 01908 761987
VAT REG GB 0745 8383 56

Account 3993        6 November 2000

| date | your reference | our reference | payment amount |
|---|---|---|---|
| 01 10 00 | INVOICE 787923 | 47609 | 277.30 |
| 10 10 00 | CREDIT NOTE 12157 | 47609 | (27.73) |
| | | **CHEQUE TOTAL** | 249.57 |

**see page 42 for an activity involving this document**

## CHEQUE – the buyer sends a payment

| | |
|---|---|
| **purpose of the document** | a payment document which, when completed, can be paid into a bank account; it enables people to settle debts, for example a buyer paying money to a seller |
| **who completes it?** | the person who owes the money signs the cheque and writes the amount in words and figures, the name of the person who is to receive the money (the payee) and the date |
| **what happens to it?** | it is passed or posted by the buyer to the seller |
| **why must it be accurate?** | if the amount is wrong the seller could end up being underpaid or overpaid; also, any mistake on the cheque could result in the banks refusing to let it through the clearing system |

**what happens in this case?**

Trends complete the details on the cheque – including the date, amount and signature – and send it to Cool Socks with the remittance advice.

**points to note:**

- If a cheque is not completed correctly, it could be refused by the banks. Particular points to note are:
  - the cheque should be signed – it is completely invalid without a signature
  - the amount in words and figures must be the same
  - lines should be drawn after the name of the payee and the amount to prevent fraud
  - the current date should be written in – cheques become invalid after six months

- The lines across the cheque are known as the 'crossing'. The words 'a/c payee only' are an important security measure because they mean that the cheque can only be paid into the account of the person named on the 'pay' line of the cheque.

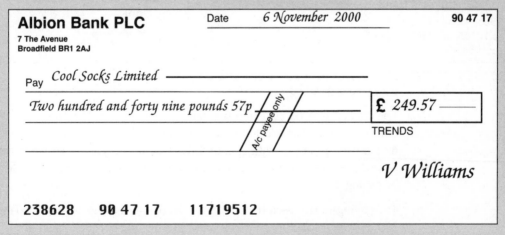

see pages 42 to 44 for activities involving this document

## paying the cheque into the bank

The flow of documents between buyer and seller is now complete.

The seller and buyer now have further financial documents to deal with because the cheque has to be banked by the seller and deducted from the bank account of the buyer:

*   the seller pays the cheque into the bank on a **paying-in slip**
*   the seller's bank will in due course send a **bank statement** to the seller showing the amount of the paying-in slip being added to the account
*   the buyer's bank will in due course send a **bank statement** to the buyer showing the amount of the cheque deducted from the bank account

The process looks like this:

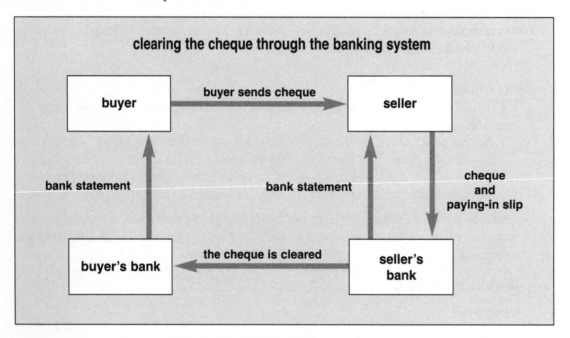

### paying-in slip

The cheque will be paid into the bank on a paying-in slip, normally with other cheques and any cash that needs paying in. Paying-in slips are provided by the bank in books with counterfoils or carbon copies. They are usually printed with the name and bank account number of the business which will be paying in.

The paying-in slip used by Cool Socks to pay in the cheque sent by Trends is shown on the next page. In this case just the one cheque is paid in.

## PAYING-IN SLIP — the seller pays the cheque into the bank

**purpose of the document**  to pay cheques and cash into a bank account

**who completes it?**  the business paying the money into the bank

**what happens to it?**  it is processed by the bank to place the money on the bank account of the business

**why must it be accurate?**  if the figures are incorrect on the paying-in slip and the bank does not pick up the error, the wrong amount may be placed on the bank account and shown on the bank statement (see page 31)

**what happens in this case?**
Cool Socks completes the paying-in slip and the counterfoil with details of
- the amount of money being paid in
- the signature of the person paying in the money
- the date that the money is paid in

The paying-in slip will be taken to the bank with the cheque and paid in over the counter. The money will normally go onto the account of Cool Socks the same day and taken off Trends' account three working days later.

**points to note:**
- If the business is also paying in cash, it is listed and totalled in the appropriate boxes on the paying-in slip and counterfoil.
- If the business is also paying in other cheques they are all listed on the back of the paying-in slip or on a tally roll and the total of the cheques is shown on the front of the paying-in slip
- If the paying-in slip is not preprinted with the business details the name of the account, the account number and the bank details (branch name and sort code number) will have to be inserted. This is very rare nowadays.

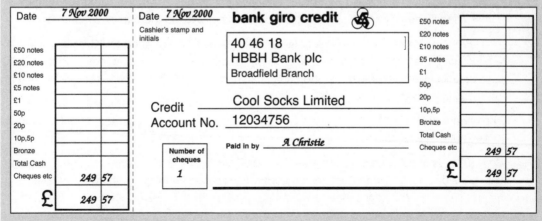

**see page 46 for an activity involving this document**

## BANK STATEMENT – a list of transactions on the bank account

| | |
|---|---|
| **purpose of the document** | to tell the business about payments in and out of the bank account and the bank balance |
| **who completes it?** | it is sent by the bank to the business |
| **what happens to it?** | the business receiving it will check all the items on it against its own records – normally kept in a 'cash book' to make sure that there are no errors |
| **why must it be accurate?** | if the bank makes a mistake (as banks sometimes do) the bank statement will differ from the records kept by the business and the bank will need to be told about any error; if the business has made an error in its financial records the bank statement will reveal this error to the business |

**what happens in this case?**
At the end of November Albion Bank sends a bank statement to Trends. Trends will check off each item in its records to pick up any errors and will write in its cash book any item it has not recorded, eg bank charges.

**points to note:**

- The bank statement is set out in columns for:

  – the date

  – columns for payments made and receipts (money received)

  – details of each transaction:
    - 'Credit' means a paying-in slip paying in money
    - The six digit numbers are cheques
    - The receipts described as 'BACS' are payments received via the banks' computers
    - The payments described as DD are payments made via the banks' computers

  – a running balance of the bank balance; the letters 'CR' are short for 'Credit'. They indicate that the bank balance is 'in credit', in other words, it has money in it. If the bank balance was overdrawn – ie the bank customer is borrowing – it would have the letters 'DR' which are short for 'Debit'.

- The cheque for £249.57 written out to Cool Socks appears on the statement on 9 November (3 days after it was paid in).

- When Trends checks the bank statement it is unlikely that its final balance will agree with the final bank balance in Trends' financial records. The reason for this is that there will be timing differences – for example cheques written out by Trends and posted off but not yet paid in and deducted from the account.

## BANK STATEMENT

**Albion Bank plc**
**7 The Avenue, Broadfield, BR1 2AJ**

**Account title** Trends

**Account number** 11719512
**Statement** 85

| Date | Details | Payments | Receipts | Balance |
|---|---|---|---|---|
| 20-0 | | | | |
| 1 Nov | Balance brought down | | | 1,678.90 CR |
| 9 Nov | Credit | | 1,427.85 | 3106.75 CR |
| 9 Nov | 238628 | 249.57 | | 2,857.18 CR |
| 10 Nov | 238629 | 50.00 | | 2,807.18 CR |
| 13 Nov | Credit | | 67.45 | 2,874.63 CR |
| 16 Nov | Credit | | 100.00 | 2,974.63 CR |
| 16 Nov | BACS HMRST 25453 | | 500.00 | 3,474.63 CR |
| 22 Nov | 238630 | 783.90 | | 2,690.73 CR |
| 23 Nov | 238626 | 127.00 | | 2,563.73 CR |
| 23 Nov | Credit | | 1,006.70 | 3,570.43 CR |
| 23 Nov | BACS ORLANDO 37646 | | 162.30 | 3,732.73 CR |
| 24 Nov | DD Westmid Gas | 167.50 | | 3,565.23 CR |
| 27 Nov | 238634 | 421.80 | | 3,143.43 CR |
| 27 Nov | DD RT Telecom | 96.50 | | 3,046.93 CR |
| 30 Nov | Bank charges | 87.50 | | 2,959.43 CR |

**transaction date**

**transaction details**

**cheque to Cool Socks**

**payments out of the account**

**payments into the account**

**running balance of the account**

**see page 46 for an activity involving this document**

## CHAPTER SUMMARY

- The stakeholders of a business need to know about the financial state of the business; this information can be found in the financial statements. The stakeholders include:
  - owners
  - managers
  - employees
  - customers
  - suppliers
  - lenders
  - investors
  - the tax authorities

- It is therefore important that the financial statements and the accounting system from which they are drawn are maintained accurately.

- The starting point of the accounting system of a business is the documentation generated by financial transactions.

- The accounting system then takes the information generated by the financial transactions through the books of the business, finally presenting it in the form of financial statements: the profit and loss statement and the balance sheet.

- A cash purchase is when someone buys something and payment is made straightaway. A credit purchase is when payment for a purchase is made at a later date. Both processes involves the issue of a number of different financial documents which 'flow' in a specific order. They are listed in the Key Terms opposite. The flow for a credit transaction can involve, for example:
  - purchase order sent by buyer
  - invoice and delivery note sent by seller
  - credit note sent by seller
  - statement of account sent by seller
  - cheque and remittance advice sent by buyer

- Financial documents must be completed accurately and checked on receipt to avoid problems such as the wrong goods being supplied or the wrong amount being charged.

- When money is received by the seller it must be paid promptly into the bank account on a paying-in slip and then checked on the bank statement when it is received.

## KEY TERMS

| | |
|---|---|
| **stakeholders** | people or bodies who have an interest in the business |

Make sure that you are familiar with and can define the following financial documents described in this chapter:

| | |
|---|---|
| **receipt** | a record of a purchase when payment is made straightaway – a document given by the seller |
| **purchase order** | sent by the buyer – the document orders the products |
| **delivery note** | sent by the seller with the goods, often signed as proof of receipt by the buyer |
| **goods received note** | an internal document completed by the buyer as a record that the goods have been received and checked |
| **invoice** | sent by the seller to the buyer advising how much is owed, for what, and when payment is due |
| **credit note** | sent by the seller to the buyer advising any deduction to be made from the amount owing |
| **statement of account** | sent by the seller to the buyer stating how much is owed, listing all invoices, credit notes and payments |
| **remittance advice** | sent by the buyer to the seller advising that payment is being made |
| **cheque** | a payment document which can be paid into a bank account |
| **paying-in slip** | a slip which lists cash and cheques being paid into the bank |
| **bank statement** | a list of payments in and out of the bank account |

Make sure that you are familiar with the following terms:

| | |
|---|---|
| **cash purchase** | a purchase where payment is made straightaway |
| **credit purchase** | a purchase where payment is made at a later date |
| **Value Added Tax (VAT)** | a tax charged by businesses on the sale of goods and services |
| **trade discount** | a percentage amount deducted from the invoice total before any VAT is added on |
| **cash discount** | a discount deducted from the invoice total after trade discount has been deducted and before VAT is added |

# 2

# Financial documents – practical exercises

### in-tray exercise

In this chapter you will practise completing and checking the financial documents explained in the last chapter. The documents used here are those used in a credit purchase and when paying money into the bank. If you need blank documents they are available on the Osborne Books website: www.osbornebooks.co.uk in the Resources section. To remind you of the 'flow' of documents that normally takes place, study the diagram shown below.

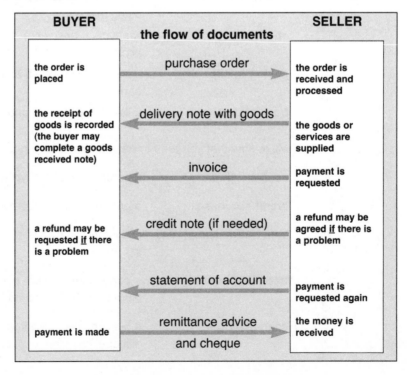

| BUYER | the flow of documents | SELLER |
|---|---|---|
| the order is placed | purchase order → | the order is received and processed |
| the receipt of goods is recorded (the buyer may complete a goods received note) | ← delivery note with goods | the goods or services are supplied |
| | ← invoice | payment is requested |
| a refund may be requested if there is a problem | ← credit note (if needed) | a refund may be agreed if there is a problem |
| | ← statement of account | payment is requested again |
| payment is made | remittance advice → and cheque | the money is received |

## Activity 2.1

# Making the purchase

Blank financial documents are available from the Resources section of the Osborne Books website: www.osbornebooks.co.uk

## task 1

Work in pairs and play the roles of buyer and seller. The buyer is a clothes shop Oasis, 5 High Street, Mereford MR1 3GF and the seller a clothes importer, Fashions Imports Limited, Unit 4 Beech Industrial Estate, Salebury, Manchester, M62 5FG. You will need copies of blank purchase orders and invoices (see note above). You should use today's date and the current VAT rate, but will need to make up the following details:

- catalogue numbers
- order numbers and invoice numbers

The buyer is to complete two separate purchase orders and the seller is to complete an invoice and a delivery note for each order. The orders are as follows:

(a)    100 pairs of tights (black) at £1.50 each
        25 sweatshirts (green) at £8 each
        50 T shirts (black) at £3.50 each

(b)    25 fleeces (red) at £15 each
        30 pairs of jeans (black) at £17.50 each
        50 pairs of tights (black) at £1.50 each

There is no trade discount available to the buyer. Add VAT at the current rate and round it down to the nearest pence.

## task 2

You work for Deansway Trading Company, a wholesaler of office stationery, which trades from The Modern Office, 79 Deansway, Stourminster WR1 2EJ. A customer, The Card Shop of 126 The Crescent, Marshall Green, WR4 5TX, orders the following on order number 9516:

(a)    50 boxes of assorted rubbers at 50p per box, catalogue no 26537

(b)    1000 shorthand notebooks at £4 for a pack of 10, catalogue no 72625

(c)    250 ring binders (red) at £2.50 each, catalogue no 72698

VAT is to be charged at the current rate on all items, and a 5% trade discount is given to The Card Shop. Prepare invoice number 8234, under today's date, to be sent to the customer. When the invoice is complete, calculate the amount due if a 2.5% cash discount is allowed for early settlement.

## Activity 2.2

# Checking invoices

## task 1

A colleague in the Accounts Department of Cool Socks has prepared this sales invoice. You are to check it and state what is wrong with it. You are then to draw up a new invoice with the same reference number and today's date. Assume the price quoted is correct.

---

## INVOICE

# COOL SOCKS LIMITED

Unit 45 Elgar Estate, Broadfield, BR7 4ER
Tel 01908 765314  Fax 01908 765951
VAT REG GB 0745 4672 76

invoice to

| | |
|---|---|
| Oasis | |
| 5 High Street | |
| Mereford | |
| MR1 3GF | |

| | |
|---|---|
| invoice no | 876512 |
| account | 3461 |
| your reference | 87541 |

date/tax point

| product code | description | quantity | price | unit | total | discount % | net |
|---|---|---|---|---|---|---|---|
| 45R | Red Toebar socks | 100 | 2.45 | pair | 254.00 | 10.00 | 279.40 |

| | |
|---|---|
| GOODS TOTAL | 279.40 |
| VAT | 48.89 |
| TOTAL | 230.51 |

terms: 30 days

## task 2

You work in the Oasis clothes shop and have received this invoice in the post. You check it against your Purchase Order, the details of which are:

Order No 98372 for 50 pairs of dark blue Country trousers @ £12.45 a pair (code 234DB). You are normally given 10% trade discount.

The jeans were received, as ordered, on the same day as the invoice.

Check the invoice against the purchase order and if there are any problems contact the Sales Ledger Department of The Jeans Company by e-mail, fax or letter. Draft out the text of your e-mail, fax or letter on a word processing file.

## INVOICE

# The Jeans Company

Unit 6 Parry Trading Estate, Southfield, SF1 5LR
Tel 01901 333391  Fax 01901 333462  email Jeansco@goblin.com
VAT REG GB 8762 54 27

invoice to

Oasis
5 High Street
Mereford
MR1 3GF

| | |
|---|---|
| invoice no | 942394 |
| account | 2141 |
| your reference | 98372 |
| date/tax point | 01 12 00 |

| product code | description | quantity | price | unit | total | discount % | net |
|---|---|---|---|---|---|---|---|
| 234B | Country trousers (black) | 50 | 12.45 | pair | 622.50 | 5.00 | 591.38 |

| | |
|---|---|
| GOODS TOTAL | 591.38 |
| VAT | 103.49 |
| TOTAL | 694.87 |

terms: 30 days

## Activity 2.3

# A goods received note is completed

You work in an insurance broker's office and have just received a consignment of 50 reams of photocopy paper from Wintergreen Stationers. A ream is a packet of 500 sheets. The reams are packed in boxes of five. One of the boxes is badly dented at one end. The 5 reams of paper in this box are unusable as they will jam any photocopier or printer. The delivery note for the paper is shown below.

---

### DELIVERY NOTE

## WINTERGREEN STATIONERS

75 Holmes Street, Broadfield, BR2 6TF
Tel 01908 342281  Fax 01908 342538  Email WGreen@newserve.com
VAT REG GB 0822 2422 75

| Uplands Insurance Brokers<br>8 Friar Street<br>Broadfield<br>BR1 3RF | delivery note no | 68673 |
| | delivery method | Parcelexpress |
| | your order | 23423 |
| | date | 02 10 00 |

| product code | quantity | description |
|---|---|---|
| A4PPW | 50 reams | A4 photocopier paper, white, 80gsm |

**Received**
signature.............*J Rutter*...............name (capitals)...*J RUTTER*.................date*5/10/00*

---

1   You are to complete a Goods Received Note. See the Osborne website: www.osbornebooks.co.uk for copies of blank documents.

   The goods arrived by Parcelexpress, consignment number 7429472

2   Why is it important that a Goods Received Note is completed? What might happen if the brokers buying the goods just sent back the damaged paper by carrier and relied solely on the delivery note for its  financial records?

The following day the invoice for the goods arrives by post. This will be dealt with in the next Activity.

## Activity 2.4

# A credit note is requested

The invoice for the photocopy paper delivered in the last Activity is shown below. It should be checked carefully for errors. Uplands Insurance Brokers normally receives a 10% discount on goods supplied.

You are to write the text of a letter (or fax or email) to the Accounts Department requesting a credit note for the returned paper. The text should include the money amount (including VAT) of the credit that is due.

---

### INVOICE

# WINTERGREEN STATIONERS

75 Holmes Street, Broadfield, BR2 6TF
Tel 01908 342281  Fax 01908 342538  Email WGreen@newserve.com
VAT REG GB 0822 2422 75

invoice to

| Uplands Insurance Brokers |
| 8 Friar Street |
| Broadfield |
| BR1 3RF |

| | |
|---|---|
| invoice no | **9384** |
| account | **3455** |
| your reference | **23423** |
| date/tax point | **02 10 00** |

| product code | description | quantity | price | unit | total | discount % | net |
|---|---|---|---|---|---|---|---|
| A4PPW | A4 photocopy paper white, 80gsm | 50 | 1.70 | ream | 85.00 | 10.00 | 76.50 |

| | |
|---|---|
| GOODS TOTAL | 76.50 |
| VAT | 13.38 |
| TOTAL | 89.88 |

terms: 30 days

## Activity 2.5

# A credit note is issued

When you have had your answer to Activity 2.4 checked you should complete the credit note issued by Wintergreen Stationers, the suppliers of the damaged paper. Do not forget the discount!

You will find a blank credit note in the Resources section of the Osborne Books website: www.osbornebooks.co.uk

## Activity 2.6

# Sending statements

It is the end of the month of October in the Accounts Department of Wintergreen Stationers. You have been asked to prepare the statements for two of your customers. Their statements for last month (issued on 29 September) are illustrated on the next page – they will be needed for the starting balance for October. You will see how the starting balance (Balance b/f) is shown on the September statements.

The transactions on the two accounts for October are shown below.

**Tiny Toys Limited**

| Date | Transaction | Amount (£) |
| --- | --- | --- |
| 10 10 00 | Payment received | 105.00 |
| 13 10 00 | Invoice 9410 | 560.00 |
| 20 10 00 | Invoice 9488 | 3450.50 |
| 26 10 00 | Credit note 12180 | 230.50 |

**R Patel Associates**

| Date | Transaction | Amount (£) |
| --- | --- | --- |
| 10 10 00 | Payment received | 4999.83 |
| 16 10 00 | Invoice 9433 | 1098.50 |
| 23 10 00 | Invoice 9501 | 678.35 |
| 26 10 00 | Credit note 12183 | 670.00 |

You will find a blank statement in the Resources section of the Osborne Books website: www.osbornebooks.co.uk

---

### STATEMENT OF ACCOUNT

# WINTERGREEN STATIONERS

75 Holmes Street, Broadfield, BR2 6TF
Tel 01908 342281  Fax 01908 342538  Email WGreen@newserve.com
VAT REG GB 0822 2422 75

TO

| Tiny Toys Limited<br>56 Broad Avenue<br>Brocknell<br>BK7 6CV | account | 3001 |
| --- | --- | --- |
| | date | 29 09 00 |

| date | details | debit<br>£ | credit<br>£ | balance<br>£ |
| --- | --- | --- | --- | --- |
| 01 09 00 | Balance b/f | | | 139.67 |
| 05 09 00 | Payment received | | 139.67 | nil |
| 19 09 00 | Invoice 9276 | 150.00 | | 150.00 |
| 25 09 00 | Credit note 12157 | | 45.00 | 105.00 |

| **AMOUNT NOW DUE** | 105.00 |
| --- | --- |

---

### STATEMENT OF ACCOUNT

# WINTERGREEN STATIONERS

75 Holmes Street, Broadfield, BR2 6TF
Tel 01908 342281  Fax 01908 342538  Email WGreen@newserve.com
VAT REG GB 0822 2422 75

TO

| R Patel Associates<br>78 Greenford Mansions<br>Mereford<br>MR3 8KJ | account | 3067 |
| --- | --- | --- |
| | date | 29 09 00 |

| date | details | debit<br>£ | credit<br>£ | balance<br>£ |
| --- | --- | --- | --- | --- |
| 01 09 00 | Balance b/f | | | 679.05 |
| 06 09 00 | Payment received | | 679.05 | nil |
| 21 09 00 | Invoice 9303 | 5345.50 | | 5345.50 |
| 25 09 00 | Credit note 12162 | | 345.67 | 4999.83 |

| **AMOUNT NOW DUE** | 4999.83 |
| --- | --- |

# Remittance advices and cheques

It is now the first week of November in the Accounts Department of Wintergreen Stationers. The October statements from suppliers are arriving in the post. Two are shown on the opposite page.

You are asked to make out a remittance advice and a cheque (ready for signing) to settle both accounts. Make up purchase order numbers. A sample cheque is shown at the bottom of this page. Blank remittance advices and cheques can be found on the Osborne Books website: www.osbornebooks.co.uk

You find the following note attached to the paperwork relating to the Hilliard & Brown Account.

---

**NOTE TO FILE**
19 October 2000

Hilliard & Brown - disputed invoice

Please note that we should not pay their invoice 3213 for £1,256.90 because the goods on the invoice have not been delivered. Please check each month when paying against their statement.

*R Otter*

Accounts Supervisor, Purchase Ledger

---

You check to see if the goods have arrived and find that they have not.

---

**Albion Bank PLC**    Date _____    90 47 17

7 The Avenue
Broadfield BR1 2AJ

Pay _____

_____

A/c payee only                    £

WINTERGREEN STATIONERY

123238    90 47 17    45195234

## STATEMENT OF ACCOUNT
# PRONTO SUPPLIES

Unit 17, Blakefield Estate, Broadfield, BR4 9TG
Tel 01908 482111  Fax 01908 482471  Email Pronto@imp.com
VAT REG GB4452 2411 21

TO

| Wintergreen Stationers<br>75 Holmes Street<br>Broadfield<br>BK2 6TF | | account | 2343 |
| --- | --- | --- | --- |
| | | date | 31 10 00 |

| date | details | debit £ | credit £ | balance £ |
| --- | --- | --- | --- | --- |
| 02 10 00 | Balance b/f | | | 234.75 |
| 05 10 00 | Payment received | | 234.75 | nil |
| 19 10 00 | Invoice 8717 | 290.75 | | 290.75 |
| 23 10 00 | Invoice 8734 | 654.10 | | 944.85 |
| 25 10 00 | Invoice 8766 | 125.00 | | 1069.85 |

| AMOUNT NOW DUE | 1069.85 |
| --- | --- |

## STATEMENT
# HILLIARD & BROWN

99 Caxton Street, Norwich, NR2 7VB
Tel 01603 342281  Fax 01603 342538  Email Hillibrown@newserve.com
VAT REG GB 4532 1121 06

TO

| Wintergreen Stationers<br>75 Holmes Street<br>Broadfield<br>BK2 6TF | | account | 2234 |
| --- | --- | --- | --- |
| | | date | 31 10 00 |

| date | details | debit £ | credit £ | balance £ |
| --- | --- | --- | --- | --- |
| 02 10 00 | Balance b/f | | | 560.00 |
| 05 10 00 | Payment received | | 560.00 | nil |
| 19 10 00 | Invoice 3213 | 1256.90 | | 1256.90 |
| 23 10 00 | Invoice 3244 | 987.60 | | 2244.50 |
| 25 10 00 | Credit note 4501 | | 135.00 | 2109.50 |

| AMOUNT NOW DUE | 2109.50 |
| --- | --- |

# Checking cheques

You work in the accounts department of Morton Components Limited. The cheques on the opposite page have been received in this morning's post.

The date is 10 November 2000.

The following notice to staff is kept in the accounts office.

---

**CHECK THE CHEQUES!**

If you receive a cheque with a mistake or something missing, it may not be accepted by the banks. If this should happen you will need to get the missing item filled in or the mistake corrected and any correction initialled by the person writing out the cheque. If the person has posted the cheque to us this means in most cases posting the cheque back again with a covering letter asking for the mistake to be corrected. Look out for these mistakes:

| mistake | what you do to correct it |
|---|---|
| there is no signature | send it back asking for a signature |
| the amount in words and figures differs | send it back asking for it to be corrected and the correction initialled |
| the name on the 'pay' line is wrong | send it back asking for it to be corrected and the correction initialled |
| the date is more than six months ago | send it back and ask for the date to be changed and the correction initialled |
| the date is missing | you can write it in! – this is the one situation where you do not have to send it back |

---

1 Examine the cheques on the opposite page and write down what is wrong with them.

2 State in each case what you would do to put matters right.

3 Explain what the consequences would be if you failed to take action on any of the cheques – what would happen to the cheque? What effect might this have on the financial situation of your business?

**(a)**

**Albion Bank PLC**
7 The Avenue
Broadfield BR1 2AJ

Date *6 November 2000*

90 47 17

Pay *Marton Computers Limited*

*Two hundred and forty nine pounds 87p*

A/c payee only

£ *249.87*

K J PLASTOW

*K J Plastow*

083772      90 47 17      11719881

**(b)**

**WESTSIDE BANK PLC**
22 Cornbury Street
Shelford SL1 2DC

Date *1 November 2000*

78 37 17

Pay *Morton Components Limited*

*One hundred and sixty five pounds only*

A/c payee only

£ *160.00*

BACCHUS LIMITED

072628      78 37 17      23487611

**(c)**

**Britannia Bank PLC**
89 High Street
Broadfield BR1 8GH

Date

33 44 07

Pay *Morton Components Limited*

*Thirty five pounds 95p*

A/c payee only

£ *35.95*

DAVIES MEDIA

*H Purcell*

987482      33 44 07      24221913

## Activity 2.9

# Paying-in slips and bank statements

You work in the Accounts Department of Cool Socks. It is 23 November and you have to pay some cash and a cheque in at the bank today. The details of the items you have to pay in are:

| | |
|---|---|
| Cheque (1 only) | £209.80 |
| £50 notes | £550.00 |
| £20 notes | £160.00 |
| £5 notes | £80.00 |
| £1 coins | £6.00 |
| 50p | £0.50 |
| 20p | £0.40 |

You are to complete a paying-in slip. A Cool Socks slip is shown below. Alternatively you can download a paying-in slip from the Resources section of the Osborne website www.osbornebooks.co.uk.

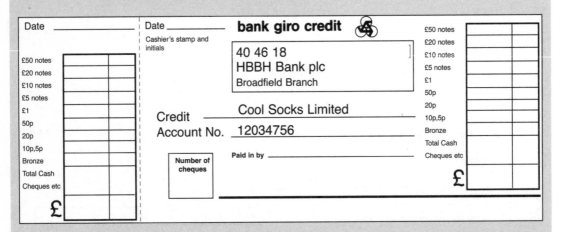

At the beginning of December you receive the bank statement shown on the next page. As part of your checking routine you would normally tally up (reconcile) the bank statement with your financial records. The records in this case are contained in the cash book which keeps a running total of items paid in and out of the bank account. The checking process involves ticking off and checking the amounts of the items that appear in both cash book and bank statement. You will also update your cash book for any items which appear in the bank statement but have not yet been entered in the cash book.

**Answer the following:**

1   Is the amount of the credit you paid in on 23 November correct?

2   What do the letters 'CR' in the right-hand column mean? What other letters could you see there?

3   The bank statement shows an item for bank charges on 30 November. This does not appear in your records. Why is this and what do you think you should do about it?

4   Two cheques – for £1,245.00 and £50.75 – do not appear on the bank statement. You wrote them out on 27 November when you were settling up the bills, entered them in your records and posted them off on that day. Why are they not on the bank statement? Are they likely to make the bank account go overdrawn?

## Albion Bank plc
**7 The Avenue, Broadfield, BR1 2AJ**

| | | Account title | Trends |
| | | Account number | 11719512 |
| | | Statement | 85 |

| Date | Details | Payments | Receipts | Balance |
|---|---|---|---|---|
| 1 Nov | Balance brought down | | | 1,678.90 CR |
| 9 Nov | Credit | | 1,427.85 | 3,106.75 CR |
| 9 Nov | 238628 | 249.57 | | 2,857.18 CR |
| 10 Nov | 238629 | 50.00 | | 2,807.18 CR |
| 13 Nov | Credit | | 67.45 | 2,874.63 CR |
| 16 Nov | Credit | | 100.00 | 2,974.63 CR |
| 16 Nov | BACS HMRST 25453 | | 500.00 | 3,474.63 CR |
| 22 Nov | 238630 | 783.90 | | 2,690.73 CR |
| 23 Nov | 238626 | 127.00 | | 2,563.73 CR |
| 23 Nov | Credit | | 1,006.70 | 3,570.43 CR |
| 23 Nov | BACS ORLANDO 37646 | | 162.30 | 3,732.73 CR |
| 24 Nov | DD Westmid Gas | 167.50 | | 3,565.23 CR |
| 27 Nov | 238634 | 421.80 | | 3,143.43 CR |
| 27 Nov | DD RT Telecom | 96.50 | | 3,046.93 CR |
| 30 Nov | Bank charges | 87.50 | | 2,959.43 CR |

# From documents to accounts

**3**

Unit 5 Business finance
Constructing accounts

## introduction

In the last two chapters we have seen what happens to the financial documents processed by a business. They form a 'flow' starting with the order and finishing with the payment. In this chapter we see how these transactions are recorded in the accounting system of the business. This system involves a 'flow' of financial data, starting with the documents, passing through the 'books' of the business and finishing up with financial statements which provide valuable information about the financial state of the business.

## what you will learn from this chapter

- financial documents such as invoices, credit notes and cheques represent sales, purchases and payments which are recorded in the first instance in 'books of original entry' such as the sales day book, purchases day book and the cash book

- financial transactions recorded in the 'books of original entry' are then in most accounting systems transferred to accounts in the double-entry book-keeping system, eg sales account, purchases account, bank account; each transaction is normally recorded in two separate accounts

- the balances of the double-entry accounts are regularly listed in a checking procedure known as the trial balance; this picks up errors in the accounting system and also forms a basis for the production of the financial statements

- the financial statements are constructed from the double-entry accounts and comprise the profit and loss account and the balance sheet

- business accounts can be operated in a paper-based system (the 'books of the business') or increasingly commonly by computer

## the accounting system

The accounting system of a business records information from documents such as invoices into the accounting records, checking that the information has been recorded correctly, and then presenting the information in financial statements which enable the owners and managers of the business to review progress.

In this chapter we look closely at the way this financial information is processed. Your external assessment may ask you to show the process in the form of a flow chart, or it may ask you to complete a flow chart. We show a summary flow chart below and will then explain the stages in more detail.

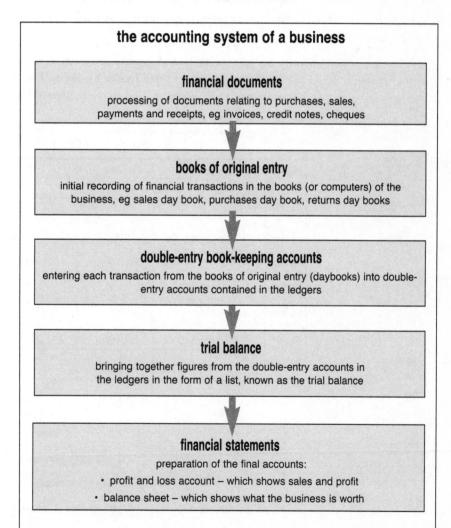

### the accounting system of a business

**financial documents**

processing of documents relating to purchases, sales, payments and receipts, eg invoices, credit notes, cheques

**books of original entry**

initial recording of financial transactions in the books (or computers) of the business, eg sales day book, purchases day book, returns day books

**double-entry book-keeping accounts**

entering each transaction from the books of original entry (daybooks) into double-entry accounts contained in the ledgers

**trial balance**

bringing together figures from the double-entry accounts in the ledgers in the form of a list, known as the trial balance

**financial statements**

preparation of the final accounts:

• profit and loss account – which shows sales and profit

• balance sheet – which shows what the business is worth

# books of original entry

The books of original entry (or 'prime entry') comprise a number of *day books* which list money amounts and other details taken from financial documents. For example the day books used for sales and purchases made on credit and involving invoices are:

> **sales day book** – compiled from sales invoices issued

> **purchases day book** – compiled from purchases invoices received

If any returns and credit notes are involved, two further day books are involved:

> **sales returns day book** – compiled from credit notes issued

> **purchases returns day book** – compiled from credit notes issued

The day books are lists of transactions which form the basis for the double-entry accounting system. A typical sales day book is shown below. As you can see it lists invoices issued by the business. The arrows explain what the items are and show how the figures are transferred to the accounts.

| Sales Day Book | | | | | |
|---|---|---|---|---|---|
| Date | Customer | Invoice No | Gross | VAT | Net |
| 2000 | | | £ | £ | £ |
| 17 Jan | R S Williams & Co | 1101 | 141.00 | 21.00 | 120.00 |
| 18 Jan | R Singh | 1102 | 188.00 | 28.00 | 160.00 |
| 20 Jan | R S Computers | 1103 | 94.00 | 14.00 | 80.00 |
| 20 Jan | K L Pitching | 1104 | 235.00 | 35.00 | 200.00 |
| 21 Jan | R S Thomas | 1105 | 141.00 | 21.00 | 120.00 |
| 31 Jan | Totals | | 799.00 | 119.00 | 680.00 |

entered in a Sales account

entered in a VAT account

the amounts entered in the customer account

the reference number of the invoice

the customer (debtor) to whom the invoice was issued

the date on which the invoice was issued

# double-entry accounts

## the accounts

The accounting system of a business is organised on the basis of a number of *accounts* which record the money amounts of financial transactions. These accounts are kept in a series of ledgers (books), either in paper-based systems or on computer. There are accounts . . .

- in the names of customers and of suppliers of the business
- for total sales and total purchases
- for VAT charged and paid out
- recording various expenses
- for items owned by the business
- for items owed by the business

You will not need to set up accounts yourself or make entries in the accounts for the purposes of this Unit, but it is useful to know what an account looks like. A typical double-entry account for a customer you are selling to on credit looks like this in a paper-based system:

| Debit | | | R S Thomas | | Credit |
|---|---|---|---|---|---|
| Date | Details | £ | Date | Details | £ |
| 2000 | | | 2000 | | |
| 6 Jan | Invoice 1007 | 100.00 | 13 Jan | Credit Note 445 | 10.00 |
| 14 Jan | Invoice 1080 | 200.00 | 20 Jan | Cheque payment | 90.00 |
| 21 Jan | Invoice 1105 | 141.00 | | | |

Note the following points:

- the name of the account is at the top – here it is the customer R S Thomas you are selling to
- the account has two sides: a debit side on the left and a credit side on the right; there are transactions in both
- the invoices issued to the customer are listed on the left-hand side – this is what the customer owes the business (he is a 'debtor' of the business)
- payments and any credit notes are listed on the right – these will reduce the amount owed by the customer
- the numerical difference between the two sides is what the customer owes in total – what is it? . . . use your calculator or your head [Answer £341]

## double-entry – debits and credits

The principle of double-entry book-keeping is that two entries are made for every financial transaction in two separate accounts:

- one entry is made on the debit (left-hand) side of one account
- the other entry is made on the credit (right-hand) side of the other account

For example, if a business pays wages, it has two accounts in which it makes entries:

- wages account – to record the amount of wages
- bank account – to record the amount of money paid out of the bank

The entries will look like this in a paper based system (the account layout has been simplified here):

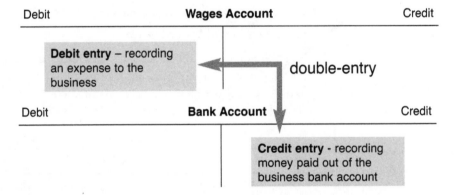

If the business was using a computer accounting program the double-entry would be carried out by entering the payment on one screen (eg the 'Bank Payments' screen) and indicating the other account on the screen by entering an account code in a required field. In simple terms, you do the entry in one account and the computer automatically does the entry in the other account.

## account balances

You will see from this double-entry process and from the account on the previous page that every account has a balance – the amount of money in it. This will obviously either be a debit balance or a credit balance.

If you study accounting (as you may do in your Options) you will practise the debit and credit entries and learn the rules for which entry goes where. For this Unit you do not need to do this, but what you do need to know is:

- that two entries (debit and credit) are needed for each transaction
- two accounts are needed for each transaction
- accounts will have either debit or credit balances, because they need to be listed in a trial balance (see later in the chapter, page 59)

# the ledger – organisation of accounts

A 'ledger' is a book in which the accounts are written up.

The term 'ledger' describes the books which are used in paper-based accounting systems. The word 'ledger' is also used in computer programs, although, of course no books are involved here – all the data is held on computer file. The major advantage of computer accounting is that it is a very accurate method of recording business transactions; the disadvantage is that it is costly to set up because it requires investment in equipment, training and back-up facilities.

## division of the ledger

Book-keepers and accountants confusingly refer to 'the ledger' when in fact they are talking about more than one book. 'The ledger' is in fact divided into a number of different ledgers. You need to know about this because each double-entry transaction may well involve two different ledgers and you will need to be able to identify in which ledgers each transaction is recorded.

The ledgers and the accounts they contain are shown in the diagram below. On the next page is an extract from a screen from a Sage computer accounting program showing how the ledgers are structured in the computer. The arrows and explanations have been added.

---

### the 'Ledger' in a paper-based accounts system

**SALES LEDGER**
contains the personal accounts of customers to whom the business has sold on credit (the 'debtors').

It records information such as:

- invoices issued
- credit notes issued
- payments received

**PURCHASES LEDGER**
contains the personal accounts of suppliers from whom the business has bought on credit (the 'creditors').

It records information such as:

- invoices received
- credit notes received
- payments sent

**GENERAL (NOMINAL) LEDGER**
contains most of the other accounts not in the Sales or Purchases Ledger. The accounts include:

- sales and purchases
- expenses and income items
- items owned (assets)
- money owed (liabilities)

**CASH BOOK**
contains:

- cash account for cash held by the business
- bank account for payments in and out of the bank account

Entries are often made in the cash book without going through a day book.

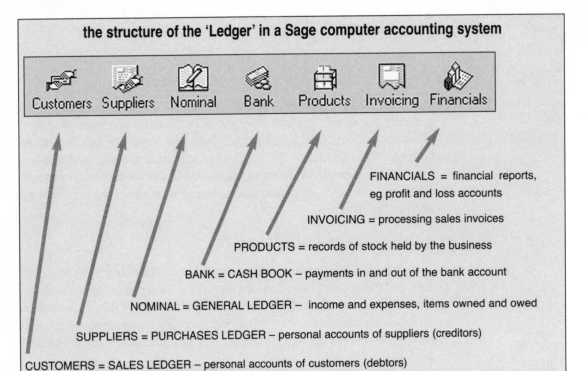

the structure of the 'Ledger' in a Sage computer accounting system

Customers   Suppliers   Nominal   Bank   Products   Invoicing   Financials

FINANCIALS = financial reports, eg profit and loss accounts

INVOICING = processing sales invoices

PRODUCTS = records of stock held by the business

BANK = CASH BOOK – payments in and out of the bank account

NOMINAL = GENERAL LEDGER – income and expenses, items owned and owed

SUPPLIERS = PURCHASES LEDGER – personal accounts of suppliers (creditors)

CUSTOMERS = SALES LEDGER – personal accounts of customers (debtors)

## Activity 3.1

# The accounting system

1   Where would you list sales invoices issued?

2   Where would you list purchases invoices received?

3   Where would you list credit notes issued?

4   Where would you list credit notes received?

5   Why is a double-entry accounting system called 'double-entry'?

What double entry accounts will you use for each of the transactions listed below? Ignore VAT. The accounts you have set up in your system include:

bank account, telephone account, computer equipment account, wages account, marketing account, sales account

6   You pay the wages for the month through the BACS.

7   You buy a new computer printer using a cheque.

8   You sell goods to a new customer who pays you straightaway by cheque.

9   You pay for an advert in the local newspaper by cheque.

10  You pay a Vodaphone bill by cheque.

# The accounting system at work

You have been asked to explain by means of flow charts how financial information 'flows' from the financial transaction involving a document, its listing in the book of original entry and its entry in two double-entry accounts in the ledgers. You can ignore VAT in your explanation. Remember that customers who owe you money are 'debtors' and suppliers to whom you owe money are 'creditors'. The accounts that you keep for them in the ledgers are 'personal accounts'.

## You issue a sales invoice for goods sold on credit to a customer

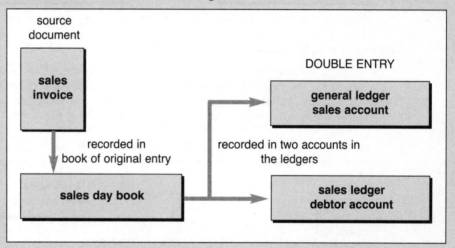

## You receive a sales invoice for goods supplied by a supplier

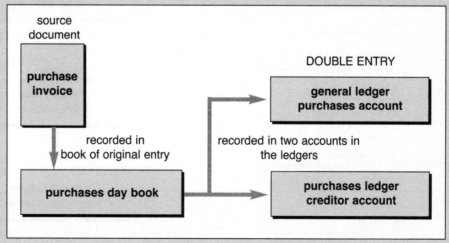

## You issue a credit note for goods returned by a customer

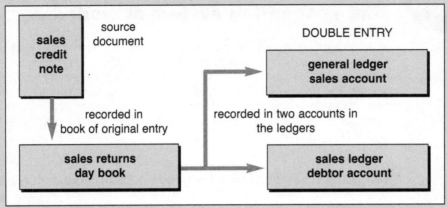

## using the cash book

This is the one exception to the rule of document ➤ book of original entry ➤ double entry accounts. The cash book, into which you enter cheques and other payments acts both as book of original entry and also as ledger. As a result any payment made or received will miss out the middle stage. Look at the following examples:

## a debtor settles up an account

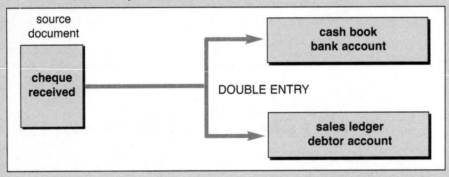

## the business pays a telephone bill

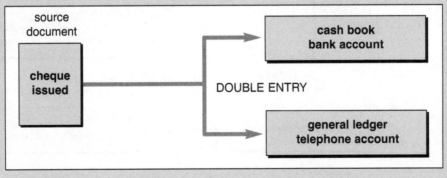

## Activity 3.2

# The accounting system

The flow diagrams shown below represent a number of financial transactions which are generated by financial documents and are eventually recorded in the double-entry accounting system. Some of the boxes have the descriptions missing.

You are to fill in the missing details, using the following:

Sales ledger (debtor account); purchases ledger (creditor account); sales day book; general ledger (sales account); general ledger (purchases account); purchases returns day book; cash book (bank account); purchase invoice; sales ledger (debtor account).

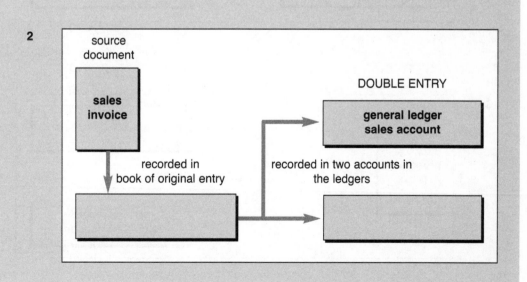

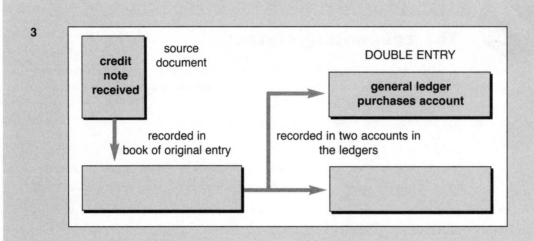

3

credit note received — source document

recorded in book of original entry

DOUBLE ENTRY

general ledger purchases account

recorded in two accounts in the ledgers

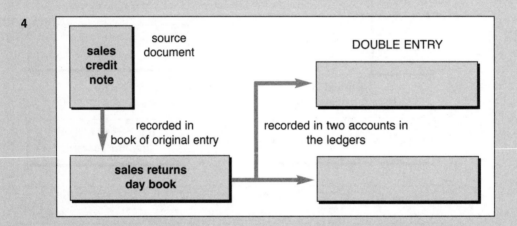

4

sales credit note — source document

recorded in book of original entry

sales returns day book

DOUBLE ENTRY

recorded in two accounts in the ledgers

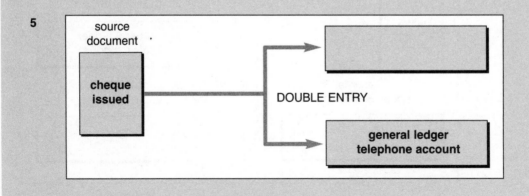

5

source document

cheque issued

DOUBLE ENTRY

general ledger telephone account

# the trial balance

A trial balance is a list of the balances of all the accounts in an accounting system. An example is shown on the next page.

The trial balance is set out in two columns (see next page for an example).

Debit balances are listed on the left and credit balances on the right; the totals of the two columns should be the same.

A trial balance lists the balance of each account in order to check the arithmetical accuracy of the accounting system.

If you think about it, if the double-entry system is worked correctly, each debit entry in an account is matched by a corresponding credit entry, so total debit entries should equal total credit entries.

## balances of accounts

The trial balance uses the balance from each double-entry account in the accounting system. By the balance of the account we mean the difference between the debit side and the credit side. (See page 51 for an account.)

You should note that certain accounts in a double-entry accounting system normally have debit balances, while others normally have credit balances.

## balances which are normally debit

These are assets (items owned) and expenses; they include:

- cash account

- purchases account (stock bought)

- fixed asset accounts, eg premises, machinery

- expense accounts, eg overheads such as power, advertising, insurance

- drawings account (which records the amount of money taken out of the business by the owner for his/her own use)

- debtors' (customers) accounts; for the purposes of a trial balance the balances of individual customer's accounts are added up, and this total is entered in the trial balance as 'debtors' – it is the total owed by customers

- stock – this represents any raw materials and items that will be sold

## balances which are normally credit

These represent liabilities (items owed by the business) and income:

- sales account

- capital account  (the amount invested in the business by the owner)

- loans to the business by banks and other lenders

- creditors' (suppliers) accounts; as with debtors the total of all the personal accounts is entered in the trial balance, not the individual balances of each account

## bank accounts – debit or credit

The bank account can either have a debit or credit balance – it will be debit when the business has money in the bank (an asset), and credit when it is overdrawn (a liability).

## example of a sole trader's trial balance

| Trial balance of Rashid Singh as at 31 December 2003 | | |
|---|---|---|
| | Debit | Credit |
| Name of account | £ | £ |
| Stock at 1 January 2003 | 12,500 | |
| Purchases | 105,000 | |
| Sales | | 155,000 |
| Administration | 6,200 | |
| Wages | 20,500 | |
| Rent paid | 3,750 | |
| Telephone | 500 | |
| Interest paid | 4,500 | |
| Travel expenses | 550 | |
| Premises | 100,000 | |
| Machinery | 20,000 | |
| Debtors | 15,500 | |
| Bank | 450 | |
| Cash | 50 | |
| Capital | | 75,000 |
| Drawings | 7,000 | |
| Loan from bank | | 50,000 |
| Creditors | | 16,500 |
| | 296,500 | 296,500 |

## notes on the trial balance

- The heading for a trial balance gives the name of the business whose accounts have been listed and the date to which it relates.

- The debit and credit columns have been totalled and the totals are the same amount. The trial balance proves that the accounts are arithmetically correct, ie debit balances equal credit balances.

- The trial balance does not, however, prove complete accuracy – for example, an item could have been recorded on the correct side, ie debit or credit, but in the wrong account. Errors like this normally surface in time: for instance, a customer (debtor) may be charged for goods sold to someone else; the customer will soon let the business know!

- A trial balance is prepared at regular intervals – often at the end of each month. The reason for this is that, if an error is found, there will be, at most, one month's book-keeping entries to check back.

- The figure for debtors has been shown as a total amount, £15,500, rather than showing the individual amounts owing by each debtor. This is quite usual and is done in order to cut down on the number of balances listed in the trial balance. The figure for creditors is shown in a similar way – as a total of the personal accounts of creditors.

## if the trial balance doesn't balance ...

If the trial balance does not balance, ie the two totals are different, there is an error (or errors):

- either in the addition of the trial balance
- and/or in the double-entry book-keeping

It will be the job of the book-keeper or accounts clerk to find the error (or errors).

## from trial balance to financial statements

As well as being a check on the arithmetical accuracy of the book-keeping the trial balance is also a starting point for the preparation of the financial statements:

- profit and loss account
- balance sheet

We will deal with this process in the next chapter.

Now carry out the Student Activities which follow in order to give you practice in extracting a trial balance.

## Activity 3.3

# Extracting trial balances

You have been given lists of account balances from two accounting systems.

You are to prepare trial balances for the two businesses, using a spreadsheet if possible.

Make sure that both trial balances are headed up with the name of the business and the date.

When you have completed them both, make sure that the totals of the columns agree.

Then answer the questions at the end of the Activity.

**Business 1: Betty Booth**

Betty Booth keeps a designer clothes shop in the town.

Her account balances as at 31 March 2003 were:

|  | £ |
|---|---|
| Stock | 10000 |
| Purchases | 127500 |
| Sales | 248610 |
| Advertising | 4900 |
| Wages | 45000 |
| Rent paid | 7000 |
| Telephone | 1200 |
| Directors salary | 31000 |
| Insurance | 4000 |
| Premises | 145000 |
| Equipment | 3950 |
| Debtors | 5120 |
| Bank (money in the account) | 5430 |
| Cash | 150 |
| Creditors | 23400 |
| Bank loan | 5000 |
| Capital | 113240 |

**Business 2: Colin Cox**

Colin Cox runs a mail order CD business.

His account balances as at 31 March 2003 were:

|  | £ |
|---|---|
| Stock | 8500 |
| Purchases | 96250 |
| Sales | 146390 |
| Advertising | 10240 |
| Wages | 28980 |
| Rent paid | 6500 |
| Telephone | 1680 |
| Interest paid | 350 |
| Travel expenses | 1045 |
| Postage | 6500 |
| Debtors | 10390 |
| Bank overdraft | 1050 |
| Cash | 150 |
| Creditors | 28950 |
| Drawings | 29450 |
| Capital | 23645 |

**tasks**

1  Produce trial balances with columns for debit and credit balances, preferably on a computer spreadsheet (see the text at the beginning of the Activity for detailed instructions).

2  In the case of Betty Booth, explain what the Debtors and Creditors figures represent, where the totals have come from and what source documents were used to compile the figures. What aspect of her business do you think makes the Debtors figure much lower than the Creditors figure?

3  How does Colin Cox's bank account balance compare with Betty Booth's bank balance? Is there any other evidence from his figures which tell you about the state of his bank balance?

## CHAPTER SUMMARY

● The accounting system of a business originates from financial transactions and the documents they generate.

● The flow of accounting information starts with the documents which are recorded in books of original entry; the data is then transfered to double - entry accounts and then to the trial balance. The information forms the basis of the financial statements of the business.

● The books of original entry – which are essentially lists of transactions – include the sales day book, purchases day book and the cash book. There are also day books for returns.

● The financial transactions recorded in the books of original entry are transferred to accounts in the double-entry book-keeping system, eg sales account, purchases account; each transaction is recorded in two separate accounts.

● The double entry accounts are constructed with a debit side (on the left) and a credit side (on the right). Each account will have a total (a 'balance') which can be calculated.

● The double entry accounts are organised in 'the Ledger'. The main ledgers are:
  - Sales Ledger, which contains the personal accounts of debtors
  - Purchases Ledger, which contains the personal accounts of creditors
  - Cash Book, which contains cash account and bank account
  - General Ledger, which contains all the other accounts, eg expenses

● An accounting system can be operated in a paper-based system or by computer. Computers tend to be more accurate and will automatically calculate account balances.

● The balances of the double-entry accounts are regularly listed in a checking procedure known as the trial balance; this picks up errors in the accounting system and also forms a basis for the production of the financial statements.

● The financial statements are constructed from the double-entry accounts and comprise the profit and loss account and the balance sheet.

## KEY TERMS

| | |
|---|---|
| **day book** | a book in which details of financial documents are listed, eg sales day book listing sales invoices issued |
| **cash book** | a book of account containing bank account and cash account; it also forms part of the Ledger (see below) |
| **double-entry** | a method of accounting in which two entries are made in the accounts for each financial transaction |
| **debit** | the left-hand side of a double-entry account |
| **debtor** | a person who owes the business money |
| **credit** | the right-hand side of a double-entry account |
| **creditor** | a person to whom the business owes money |
| **account balance** | the numerical difference between the two sides of a double-entry account |
| **ledger** | a book in which the double entry accounts are entered (the term can equally apply to a set of records held on a computer accounting program) |
| **sales ledger** | the personal accounts of customers ('debtors') who owe money to the business |
| **purchases ledger** | the personal accounts of suppliers ('creditors') who are owed money by the business |
| **general ledger** | also called 'Nominal' Ledger – contains the remaining accounts, eg expenses, income, items owned and owed |
| **trial balance** | a two-column listing of the balances of all the double-entry accounts; one column lists debit balances, the other column lists credit balances |
| **financial statements** | these are compiled regularly from the double-entry accounts and comprise: |

- a profit and loss account

- a balance sheet

# 4

# Financial statements

## introduction

When a business has extracted a trial balance from its accounting records and verified that the accounts are accurate it can then draw up its financial statements – the profit and loss account and the balance sheet. The profit and loss account shows how profitable the business is and the balance sheet gives a picture of its financial 'health' and value.

## what you will learn from this chapter

● the trial balance is the starting point for the construction of the financial statements of a business

● the profit and loss account summarises the revenues and expenses of a business and shows whether the business has made a profit or a loss over a specific period of time

● the gross profit in the profit and loss account shows the trading profit achieved; the net profit shows the profit after overheads have been deducted

● the balance sheet shows the assets (items owned), liabilities (items owed) and capital of a business at a particular date

● the assets in a balance sheet are either short-term current assets such as stock or long-term fixed assets such as machinery

● the liabilities in a balance sheet are either current liabilities (due within a year) or long-term liabilities such as bank loans

● working capital is the difference between current assets and current liabilities, capital is the investment of the owner(s)

● businesses often reduce the value of their fixed assets over time – a process known as depreciation

# the trial balance and the final accounts

As we saw in the previous chapter, the trial balance is prepared from a list of the balances on all accounts in the ledger. The trial balance proves the arithmetical accuracy of the accounting data. It also forms the basis for the preparation of financial statements from the double-entry accounts. The statements are the profit and loss account and balance sheet.

This is the trial balance from the last chapter, plus a note about stock.

| Trial balance of Rashid Singh as at 31 December 2003 | | |
|---|---|---|
| | Debit | Credit |
| Name of account | £ | £ |
| Stock at 1 January 2003 | 12,500 | |
| Purchases | 105,000 | |
| Sales | | 155,000 |
| Administration | 6,200 | |
| Wages | 20,500 | |
| Rent paid | 3,750 | |
| Telephone | 500 | |
| Interest paid | 4,500 | |
| Travel expenses | 550 | |
| Premises | 100,000 | |
| Machinery | 20,000 | |
| Debtors | 15,500 | |
| Bank | 450 | |
| Cash | 50 | |
| Capital | | 75,000 |
| Drawings | 7,000 | |
| Loan from bank | | 50,000 |
| Creditors | | 16,500 |
| | 296,500 | 296,500 |

Note: stock at 31 December 2003 was valued at £10,500

In order to prepare the financial statements of a business using a trial balance, we need to decide where all the figures will be used. For example we need to identify the assets and liabilities, and the expenses and revenue amounts. These are shown in the trial balance as either debit or credit balances.

## debit balances

These comprise assets of the business (items owned), and expenses representing the total of purchases made and the cost of overheads for the year. The debit money column indicates that this business has made purchases of goods at a cost of £105,000 during the year, while wages is an overhead, a cost to the business of £20,500. The balances for premises, machinery, stock, debtors, cash and bank indicate, in money terms, an asset of the business. The debtors' figure includes the individual balances of all the firm's debtors, ie those customers who owe money to the firm.

## credit balances

These comprise liabilities of the business (items owed), and revenue (income) amounts, including the total of sales made. For example, the sales figure shows the total amount of goods that has been sold by the business during the year. The figures for owner's capital, loan from the bank and the creditors shows the amount of the liability at the trial balance date. The creditors figure includes all the individual balances of the business' creditors, ie those suppliers to whom the business owes money.

## treatment of stock

Stock means the materials and items which the business holds which it intends to sell. Stock obviously has a money value for the business. The question is, how is it recorded in the accounting records? You will see that the trial balance debit column includes an item for the stock value at the start of the year, while the end-of-year valuation is noted after the trial balance. For the purposes of financial statements, the stock of goods is valued by the business (and often verified by the auditor) at the end of each financial year. The year-end stock value is noted at the end of the trial balance because it does not, at this stage, form part of the accounting records – it is just stock that has been counted and valued. The valuation is entered into the accounting system when the final accounts are prepared.

## the trial balance and final accounts

We can now indicate against each figure from the trial balance, in a column to the right, which financial statement it will appear in:

- expenses and revenue appear in the profit and loss account (abbreviated to 'P&L')
- assets and liabilities appear in the balance sheet (abbreviated to 'BS')

If this routine is carried out with the trial balance of Rashid Singh, it will then appear as follows:

| Trial balance of Rashid Singh as at 31 December 2003 | | | |
| --- | --- | --- | --- |
| | Debit | Credit | |
| Name of account | £ | £ | |
| Stock at 1 January 2003 | 12,500 | | P&L |
| Purchases | 105,000 | | P&L |
| Sales | | 155,000 | P&L |
| Administration | 6,200 | | P&L |
| Wages | 20,500 | | P&L |
| Rent paid | 3,750 | | P&L |
| Telephone | 500 | | P&L |
| Interest paid | 4,500 | | P&L |
| Travel expenses | 550 | | P&L |
| Premises | 100,000 | | BS |
| Machinery | 20,000 | | BS |
| Debtors | 15,500 | | BS |
| Bank | 450 | | BS |
| Cash | 50 | | BS |
| Capital | | 75,000 | BS |
| Drawings | 7,000 | | BS |
| Loan from bank | | 50,000 | BS |
| Creditors | | 16,500 | BS |
| | 296,500 | 296,500 | |

Stock at 31 December 2003 was valued at £10,500  P&L and BS

Note: P&L = profit and loss account; BS = balance sheet

## a note on the stock figures

It is only the stock at the end of the year (the closing stock) that is shown as an asset in the balance sheet.

As you will see in the next section, we use the value of the stock at the start of the year (the opening stock) from the trial balance, and the closing stock to help us calculate a figure called cost of sales, which is used in the profit and loss account.

Thus the closing stock at the end of a year appears twice in the financial statements – firstly in the profit and loss account, and secondly in the balance sheet.

# Linking the trial balance to financial statements

The following trial balance has been extracted from the accounting records of Guy Wainright at 31 December 2003:

**Trial balance of Guy Wainright as at 31 December 2003**

| Name of account | Debit £ | Credit £ |
|---|---|---|
| Stock at 1 January 2003 | 25,000 | |
| Purchases | 210,000 | |
| Sales | | 310,000 |
| Administration costs | 12,400 | |
| Wages | 47,000 | |
| Rent paid | 1,500 | |
| Telephone | 1,000 | |
| Interest paid | 9,000 | |
| Travel expenses | 1,100 | |
| Premises | 200,000 | |
| Machinery | 40,000 | |
| Debtors | 31,000 | |
| Bank | 900 | |
| Cash | 100 | |
| Capital | | 150,000 |
| Drawings | 14,000 | |
| Loan from bank | | 100,000 |
| Creditors | | 33,000 |
| | 593,000 | 593,000 |

Note: Stock at 31 December 2003 was valued at £21,000

**task**

Mark against each figure from the trial balance (and also the closing stock) the financial statement – profit and loss account, balance sheet – in which it will appear.

This information will be used in the next Student Activity to construct the financial statements of Guy Wainright.

# profit and loss account

## a definition

*A profit and loss account is a financial statement which summarises the revenue and expenses of a business for an accounting period and shows the overall profit or loss.*

The profit and loss account – also known as the profit statement – uses information from the accounting records as shown by the trial balance:

- the sales (or turnover) of the business
- the purchases made by the business
- the overheads of running the business, such as administration, wages, rent paid, telephone, interest paid, travel expenses

The amount of sales is the revenue of the business, while the amounts of purchases and overheads are the expenses of the business. Look at the layout of the example of a profit and loss account on the next page.

## the accounting period

The profit and loss account covers a set period of time – an accounting period – frequently a year of business activity. Businesses produce annual accounts as a matter of course, and as you will know from your investigations, the annual accounts of public limited companies are widely available. Often the financial year-end is the same as the calendar year-end, ie 31 December. You will also encounter other year-end dates. Sole traders sometimes choose 31 March because the tax year ends on 5 April.

Businesses may also produce financial statements such as the profit and loss account at regular intervals during the year as an aid to financial management. If a computer accounting program is used, it is a simple matter of printing it out from the financial reports menu (or icon).

The important point to remember is that the accounting period must be stated in the heading of the profit and loss account.

## layout of a profit and loss account

In broad terms, the profit and loss account consists of a calculation:

REVENUE less EXPENSES  =  PROFIT or LOSS

If revenue is greater than expenses, then the business has made a profit; if expenses are greater than revenue, then a loss has been made.

**Profit and loss account
of Rashid Singh for the year ended 31 December 2003**

| | £ | £ |
|---|---|---|
| Sales | | 155,000 |
| Opening stock (1 January 2003) | 12,500 | |
| Purchases | 105,000 | |
| | 117,500 | |
| Less Closing stock (31 December 2003) | 10,500 | |
| Cost of Sales | | 107,000 |
| Gross profit | | 48,000 |
| Less overheads: | | |
| Administration | 6,200 | |
| Wages | 20,500 | |
| Rent paid | 3,750 | |
| Telephone | 500 | |
| Interest paid | 4,500 | |
| Travel expenses | 550 | |
| | | 36,000 |
| Net profit | | 12,000 |

### format

The account is presented in a vertical format, ie it runs down the page. Two columns are used for money amounts: the right-hand column contains sub-totals and totals, while the left-hand column is used for listing individual amounts (eg overheads) which are then totalled and carried to the right-hand column.

### cost of sales calculation

Cost of Sales represents the cost to the business of the goods which have been sold in this financial year. Cost of sales is:

    opening stock   (stock bought previously)

    + purchases   (purchased during the year)

    − closing stock   (stock left unsold at the end of the year)

    = cost of sales   (cost of what has actually been sold)

## purchases and sales

The amounts for sales and purchases include only items in which the business trades. For example, a shoe shop buying shoes from the manufacturers records what it pays the manufacturers for shoes in its purchases account. The 'purchases' amount in the trial balance is the balance of the purchases account. When the shoes are sold the amount is recorded in the sales account and shown on the trial balance as 'sales'. By contrast, items bought for use in the business, such as a new till for the shop, are not included with purchases but are shown as assets on the other financial statement, the balance sheet.

## gross profit and net profit

As this is a trading business which buys and sells goods, the statement shows two levels of profit: gross profit and net profit. If it were a service sector business, such as a secretarial agency, or an accountancy firm, it will show only a net profit or loss, because it does not buy and sell goods but provides a service.

Gross profit is calculated as:

$$\text{SALES minus COST OF SALES} = \text{GROSS PROFIT}$$

If cost of sales is greater than sales, the business has made a gross loss. This would be rather unusual!

Net profit is calculated as:

$$\text{GROSS PROFIT minus OVERHEADS} = \text{NET PROFIT}$$

If overheads are more than gross profit, the business has made a net loss.

## overheads

The overheads are the running costs of the business, for example administration, wages, rent paid, telephone, interest paid, travel expenses.

## what happens to net profit?

The net profit is the amount the business has earned for the owner(s) during the year, and is subject to taxation. The owner(s) can draw some or all of the net profit for personal use – the accounting term for this is drawings. However, it might be that part of the profit will be left in the business in order to help build up the business for the future.

The example profit and loss account shown opposite is for a sole trader, ie one person in business. For other business units, such as partnerships and limited companies, the profit and loss account will show how the net profit is shared amongst the owners of the business – an agreed share of profits to each partner or dividends to shareholders.

## balance sheet

*A balance sheet is a financial statement which shows the assets, liabilities and capital of a business at a particular date.*

Balance sheets are different from profit and loss accounts which show profits for a time period such as a year. Balance sheets show the state of the business at one moment in time – things could be somewhat different tomorrow. A balance sheet is often described as a 'snapshot' of a business at one moment in time.

The money amounts of these assets, liabilities, and capital are taken from the accounting records of the business.

The balance sheet lists:

### assets

Assets are amounts owned by the business, such as premises, vehicles, stock for resale, debtors (amounts owed by customers), cash, money in the bank.

### liabilities

Liabilities are amounts owed by the business, such as creditors (amounts owed by the business to suppliers), any bank overdraft and loans.

### capital

The capital is the amount of the owner's finance put into the business and profits built up over the years.

### layout of the balance sheet

The balance sheet shows the value of the assets used by the business to make profits and how they have been financed. This concept may be expressed as follows:

ASSETS minus LIABILITIES  = CAPITAL

The balance sheet shows the asset strength of the business, in contrast to the profit and loss account, which shows the profits from the trading activities.

A more detailed example of a balance sheet, using the figures from Rashid Singh's trial balance (page 69) is shown on the next page. Note that it is presented in a vertical format, and assets and liabilities are listed under the headings of fixed assets, current assets, current liabilities, long-term liabilities, and capital: these terms are explained in detail after the balance sheet.

### Balance sheet of Rashid Singh as at 31 December 2003

|  | £ | £ |
|---|---|---|
| **Fixed assets** | | |
| Premises | | 100,000 |
| Machinery | | 20,000 |
| | | 120,000 |
| **Current assets** | | |
| Stock | 10,500 | |
| Debtors | 15,500 | |
| Bank | 450 | |
| Cash | 50 | |
| | 26,500 | |
| **Less Current liabilities** | | |
| Creditors | 16,500 | |
| **Working capital** | | 10,000 |
| | | 130,000 |
| **Less Long-term liabilities** | | |
| Loan from bank | | 50,000 |
| **NET ASSETS** | | 80,000 |
| **FINANCED BY** | | |
| **Capital** | | |
| Opening capital | | 75,000 |
| Add net profit | | 12,000 |
| | | 87,000 |
| Less drawings | | 7,000 |
| | | 80,000 |

We will now explain each of the main headings, starting from the top of the balance sheet.

## fixed assets

These comprise the long-term items owned by a business which are not bought with the intention of selling them off in the near future, eg premises, machinery, vehicles, office equipment, furniture, etc. When a business buys new fixed assets, such expenditure is called capital expenditure (in contrast to revenue expenditure which is the cost of the business' overheads shown in the profit and loss account).

### current assets

These comprise short-term assets which change regularly, eg stocks of goods for resale, debtors (amounts owed to the business by customers), bank balances and cash. These items will alter as the business trades, eg stocks will be sold, or more will be bought; debtors will make payment to the business, or sales on credit will be made; the cash and bank balances will alter with the flow of money paid into the bank account, or as withdrawals are made.

By tradition, fixed and current assets are listed from the top, starting with the most permanent, ie premises, and working through to the most liquid, ie nearest to cash: either cash itself, or the balance at the bank.

### current liabilities

These are liabilities (items owed) which are due for repayment within twelve months of the date of the balance sheet, eg creditors (amounts owed by the business to suppliers), and bank overdraft.

### working capital

This is the excess of current assets over current liabilities, ie current assets minus current liabilities = working capital. Without adequate working capital, a business will find it difficult to continue to operate (see Chapter 2 on page 34) as it may find it cannot pay its bills.

### long-term liabilities

These liabilities represent loans to the business where repayment is due in more than one year from the date of the balance sheet; they are often described as 'bank loan', 'long-term loan', or 'mortgage'.

### net assets

This section shows the actual amount of assets used by the business, ie fixed and current assets minus current and long-term liabilities. The net assets are financed by the owner(s) of the business, in the form of capital. The total of the net assets therefore equals the total of the 'financed by' section – the balance sheet 'balances'.

### capital

Capital is the owner's investment, and is a liability of a business, ie it is what the business owes the owner. It is important to realise that the assets and liabilities of a business are treated separately from the personal assets and liabilities of the owner of the business. For example, if a group of people decided to set up in business they would each agree to put in a certain amount of capital to start the business. As individuals they regard their capital as an investment, ie an asset which may, at some time, be repaid to them. From the point of view of the business, the capital is a liability, because it is owed to the owner or owners. In practice, it is unlikely to be repaid as it is the permanent capital of the business.

To the owner's capital is added net profit for the year, while drawings, the amount withdrawn by the owner during the year, are deducted, ie:

|  | owner's capital | (from the trial balance) |
|---|---|---|
| plus | net profit for the year | (from the profit & loss account) |
| minus | owner's drawings for the year | (from the trial balance) |
| equals | closing capital | |

This calculation leaves a closing capital at the balance sheet date which balances (agrees) with the net assets figure – the balance sheet balances. (Please note that drawings must not be included amongst the overheads in the profit and loss account).

In partnership balance sheets the same details, ie capital, net profit, and drawings, are shown for each partner, together with other items which relate specifically to the way in which the partners have agreed to share profits and losses.

In limited company balance sheets (see later in the chapter), details of the share capital issued by the company are shown, together with retained profits for the year, ie profit after payment of dividends to the shareholders.

## production of financial statements

In the last few pages we have looked at the layout of the profit and loss account and the balance sheet. We now need to see how these financial statements are produced, using the trial balance as the starting point.

Against each figure from the trial balance we indicate whether it will appear in the profit and loss account ('P&L') or the balance sheet ('BS'). Look at the trial balance of Rashid Singh page 69 to see how this has been done. Note that the stock at the end of the year (which appears as a note to the trial balance) is marked to appear in both 'P&L' and 'BS'.

### profit and loss account

The figures from the trial balance that have been marked 'P&L' (see page 69) are now entered onto the profit and loss account. The procedure is as follows:

- enter the sales figures in the right-hand money column
- now calculate the cost of sales in the left-hand money column, taking care to add the opening stock and to deduct the closing stock; work out the total (for Rashid Singh, it is £107,000), and carry it into the right-hand column
- deduct cost of sales from sales to give the figure for gross profit
- in the left-hand money column list the overheads of the business, work out the total (for Rashid Singh, it is £36,000), and carry it into the right-hand column
- deduct the total of overheads from gross profit to give the figure for net profit

As we have seen earlier, the right-hand money column contains sub-totals and totals, while the left-hand column is used for listing individual amounts.

### balance sheet

For the balance sheet, all figures are entered in the right-hand money column, unless we want to calculate some intermediate figures – see the example of Rashid Singh's balance sheet on page 75. Using the items from the trial balance marked 'BS', work as follows:

- list the fixed assets and sub-total
- list the current assets in the left-hand money column and sub-total in the same column (for Rashid Singh, the figure is £26,500)
- write down the current liabilities and, if there is more than one, sub-total in the left-hand money column
- deduct current liabilities from current assets to give the working capital figure (£10,000 for Rashid Singh) and carry it into the right-hand column
- in the right-hand money column, add together the sub-total of fixed assets and working capital (to give £130,000 for Rashid Singh); from this figure deduct long-term liabilities (if any), to give a final 'net assets' figure (£80,000 for Rashid Singh)

Now complete the balance sheet by filling in the figures for the 'financed by' section:

- opening capital is from the trial balance
- net profit is the figure from the profit and loss account; it is added to opening capital and sub-totalled (£87,000 for Rashid Singh)
- deduct the figure for owner's drawings to give the total of the 'financed by' section, which balances with 'net assets' (£80,000 for Rashid Singh)

*Spend a little time reading through and understanding the example of Rashid Singh's business, and then move on to the Student Activity which follows.*

## Activity 4.2

# Production of financial statements
# Guy Wainright & Jane Hayes

**task 1**

Please refer back to Activity 4.1 You should have already marked up the items from the trial balance of Guy Wainright according to whether they will appear in the profit and loss account or balance sheet. The trial balance is shown below for reference.

When your workings have been checked by your tutor, prepare the financial statements (profit and loss account and balance sheet) of Guy Wainright's business for the year ended 31 December 2003.

**Trial balance of Guy Wainright as at 31 December 2003**

| Name of account | Debit £ | Credit £ |
|---|---|---|
| Stock at 1 January 2003 | 25,000 | |
| Purchases | 210,000 | |
| Sales | | 310,000 |
| Administration costs | 12,400 | |
| Wages | 47,000 | |
| Rent paid | 1,500 | |
| Telephone | 1,000 | |
| Interest paid | 9,000 | |
| Travel expenses | 1,100 | |
| Premises | 200,000 | |
| Machinery | 40,000 | |
| Debtors | 31,000 | |
| Bank | 900 | |
| Cash | 100 | |
| Capital | | 150,000 |
| Drawings | 14,000 | |
| Loan from bank | | 100,000 |
| Creditors | | 33,000 |
| | 593,000 | 593,000 |

Note: Stock at 31 December 2003 was valued at £21,000

**see next page**

## task 2

The trial balance of Jane Hayes, who runs a bookshop, has been extracted at the end of her financial year on 30 June 2003, as follows:

| Name of account | Debit £ | Credit £ |
|---|---|---|
| Stock at 1 July 2002 | 13,250 | |
| Capital | | 70,000 |
| Premises | 65,000 | |
| Motor vehicle | 5,250 | |
| Purchases | 55,000 | |
| Sales | | 85,500 |
| Administration | 850 | |
| Wages | 9,220 | |
| Rent paid | 1,200 | |
| Telephone | 680 | |
| Interest paid | 120 | |
| Travel expenses | 330 | |
| Debtors | 1,350 | |
| Creditors | | 7,550 |
| Bank | 2,100 | |
| Cash | 600 | |
| Drawings | 8,100 | |
| | 163,050 | 163,050 |

Note: Stock at 30 June 2003 was valued at £18,100

(a) Using the trial balance, you are to prepare the financial statements (profit and loss account and balance sheet) of Jane Hayes' business for the year ended 30 June 2003.

(b) You are to provide an explanation to Jane of what each financial statement represents and write a note on each of the following terms:

- cost of sales
- net profit
- fixed assets
- current liabilities
- capital
- drawings

# depreciation of fixed assets

In your investigations into final accounts (financial statements) of businesses you may come across references to 'depreciation', either among the overheads in the profit and loss account or in the fixed asset section of the balance sheet. Your course does not require you to study depreciation in depth, but you do need to know what the term means when it appears in the final accounts.

*Depreciation is the estimate of the amount of the loss in value of fixed assets over a specified time period.*

Fixed assets, for example vehicles and computers, reduce in value – or depreciate – as time goes by for a number of reasons:

- **passage of time** – as they get older, their value drops
- **wear and tear** – they get old and things go wrong with them, particularly if there is a lack of maintenance
- **obsolescence** – equipment can get out of date, for example computers and communications equipment

If you buy a new car on Thursday you will not be able to sell it for the same price the following Thursday; it will have dropped in value – depreciated – by a substantial amount in that time.

## recording depreciation in financial statements

To provide a more accurate view of the financial state of a business, depreciation of fixed assets is recorded in the financial statements as follows:

- include the amount of depreciation for the year as an overhead in profit and loss account; the effect of this is to reduce the net profit
- the value of fixed assets shown in the balance sheet is reduced to reflect the amount that they have depreciated since the assets were bought

The reason for making these adjustments for depreciation is that the business has had the use of the fixed assets during the year: the estimated fall in value of the assets is recorded in profit and loss account, which now shows a more accurate profit figure while, in the balance sheet, fixed assets are reduced in value to indicate their approximate 'true' value.

## an example of depreciation in financial statements

Rashid Singh tells you that he wishes you to show £2,000 for depreciation of machinery in his financial statements for 2003. As a result he will include an overhead for 'depreciation' of £2,000 in his profit and loss account. In the balance sheet the £2,000 will reduce the value of the machinery ...

| Balance sheet of Rashid Singh as at 31 December 2003 (extract) | | | |
| --- | --- | --- | --- |
| | £ | £ | £ |
| **Fixed Assets** | Cost | Depreciation to date | Net |
| Premises | 100,000 | – | 100,000 |
| Machinery | 20,000 | 2,000 | 18,000 |
| | 120,000 | 2,000 | 118,000 |

## calculating depreciation

Rashid has said that he wants depreciation for the year of £2,000. How is this figure arrived at? There are two main ways of calculating depreciation: straight line (fixed amount each year) and reducing balance (reduced amount each year):

### straight line depreciation

This reduces the value of the asset by the same fixed amount each year. It is easily calculated:

annual depreciation $\quad = \quad \dfrac{\text{the cost of the asset}}{\text{the number of years the asset is expected to last}}$

Rashid has used this method. He expects his machinery, which cost £20,000, to last for 10 years. His calculation is:

$\dfrac{\text{the cost of the asset (£20,000)}}{\text{10 years}}$ = annual depreciation of £2,000

### reducing balance depreciation

If you buy an asset such as a car you will find that it depreciates more in the first year than in the second year. First year depreciation on a car can be as much as 40% of its value! In order to reflect this type of depreciation in the accounts a 'reducing balance' method is used. This applies a set percentage reduction to the value of the asset (the 'reduced' value) at the end of each year. With this method the depreciation amount itself goes down – reduces – each year.

If you buy an asset for £10,000 and reduce its value by 20% a year the depreciation calculation for the first two years would be:

| | | | | |
|---|---|---|---|---|
| Year 1 | £10,000 x 20% | | = | £2,000 |
| Year 2 | £8,000 (this is £10,000 minus the Year 1 £2,000 depreciation) x 20% | | = | £1,600 |

You can see that in the second year the depreciation is only £1,600 compared with £2,000 in the first year.

## Activity 4.3

# Calculating depreciation

John Silver is starting up an antiques business. He is buying a new estate car for £20,000 to carry his antiques around in and a new computer and printer for £2,000.

These are his only fixed assets. His accountant has advised him to depreciate these assets using the following methods:

*   depreciate the vehicle using 25% reducing balance depreciation
*   depreciate the computer equipment using 25% straight line depreciation

You are to:

1   Calculate the depreciation amounts for the first two years, using the figures given and the methods stated.

2   Draw up the fixed assets section of his balance sheet for the two years, assuming he has not bought any further fixed assets.

Use the following format as a guide. The question marks represent the missing figures.

| Fixed Assets | Cost £ | Depreciation to date £ | Net £ |
|---|---|---|---|
| Vehicle | 20,000 | ?? | ?? |
| Computer equipment | 2,000 | ?? | ?? |
| | 22,000 | ?? | ?? |

## using the financial statements

In this chapter we have concentrated on constructing the financial statements. In the next chapter we turn to the interpretation of financial statements by the various stakeholders of the business.

## CHAPTER SUMMARY

- The profit and loss account and the balance sheet are the principal financial statements of a business.

- The trial balance with its debit and credit columns contains all the figures, apart from the year-end stock valuation, for the construction of the financial statements of a business. The figures are mixed together and so will need to be identified for use in either statement.

- The business will need to value its stock at the end of the financial period because the figure will be needed in the balance sheet.

- The profit and loss account shows the profit or loss made by a business over an accounting period (normally a year).

- The gross profit in the profit and loss account of a business which sells a manufactured product shows the trading profit achieved. This is the sales figure minus the cost of sales total (the cost of the goods which have actually been sold in the accounting period).

- The net profit shows the profit after overheads have been deducted. In the case of a trading company it is calculated as gross profit less overheads.

- The net profit is the profit earned by the owner of the business, and is taxable. The owner can take it out of the business or use it in the business.

- The balance sheet shows the assets (items owned), liabilities (items owed) and capital of a business at a particular date in time. The formula is:

  Assets minus Liabilities equals Capital.

- The assets in a balance sheet are either short-term current assets such as stock, debtors, cash and money in the bank, or long-term fixed assets such as machinery.

- Depreciation is the process by which a business reduces the value of its fixed assets over time; depreciation can be straight-line or reducing balance.

- The liabilities in a balance sheet are either current liabilities (due within a year) or long-term liabilities such as bank loans.

- Working capital is the difference between current assets and current liabilities and is the funding which enables the business to carry on its day-to-day operations.

- Capital is the investment of the owner in the business and can include profits which have built up over time.

## KEY TERMS

| | |
|---|---|
| **profit and loss account** | a financial statement which measures the profit made by a business over an accounting period |
| **balance sheet** | a financial statement which shows at any one time how a business is financed, its working capital position and the owner's capital |
| **closing stock** | a calculation of the valuation of stock at the end of the accounting period |
| **cost of sales** | the cost to a trading business of the value of the stock actually sold during the accounting period, calculated as opening stock plus purchases minus closing stock |
| **gross profit** | trading profit: sales minus cost of sales |
| **net profit** | owner's profit: gross profit less overheads |
| **overheads** | the running costs of the business |
| **current assets** | items owned by a business for the short term |
| **fixed assets** | items owned by a business over the long term |
| **current liabilities** | items owed by a business and due for repayment within twelve months |
| **long-term liabilities** | items owed by a business and not due for repayment within twelve months |
| **working capital** | short-term funds used to finance the day-to-day operations of the business: current assets minus current liabilities |
| **net assets** | total assets less current liabilities – what the business is worth – equal to capital |
| **capital** | the investment by the owner in a business |
| **depreciation** | the estimated fall in value of fixed assets over time as a result of wear and tear, obsolescence and the passage of time, calculated as:<br>- straight line depreciation: a fixed amount each year<br>- reducing balance depreciation: a percentage of the value at the end of each year |

# 5

# Interpreting financial information

## introduction

Stakeholders in a business need to assess – for a variety of different reasons – the financial performance of a business. This is carried out by examining the figures in the financial statements of the business and calculating and analysing ratios derived from the figures. The main areas of interest to stakeholders are the profitability of a business, its ability to pays its debts and the way it works on a day-to-day basis.

## what you will learn from this chapter

- many different stakeholders have an interest in the financial performance of a business

- the main documents for providing financial information to stakeholders are the profit and loss account and the balance sheet

- the accounting ratios that measure solvency (the ability of a business to repay its debts) analyse the working capital position on the balance sheet

- profitability ratios analyse the relationship of various measures of profit against figures including sales and capital

- performance ratios examine areas such as the length of time for which stock is held and the period of time customers take to pay their invoices

- investors in public limited companies will also be interested in financial indicators such as the share price and the return on investment received in the form of dividends

# financial information for stakeholders

As we saw at the start of Chapter 1 all businesses have stakeholders who have an interest in that business. These stakeholders include:

- people inside the business – owners, managers and employees
- people the business deals with on a day-to day business – its customers and its suppliers
- people who want to lend money to the business
- investors who want to put their money into the business
- the general public
- organisations that want to ensure that the business is being run correctly and according to the regulations laid down in law

We will now look at the users of accounting information in more detail and explain what sort of financial information stakeholders are asking for.

## the owners

Whether the business is a small sole trader enterprise or a public limited company (where the owners are its shareholders), the owners will want to know how the business is performing in terms of sales and profitability, and whether it is solvent, in other words whether it can repay its debts.

## the managers

The management of a business will want to know the financial state of the business as they will have to take day-to-day decisions on the basis of the information. Managers will therefore look at:

- performance against forecast targets – sales, expenses, profit
- ways in which they can improve that performance
- control of the money coming in and out of the business – paying debts and getting customers to pay

## employees

The employer will want to motivate the employee and instill loyalty and provide job stability by showing that the business is profitable.

## customers and suppliers

Customers that buy from a business will want to be reassured that the business is financially stable so that the product will be of good quality and that the business will still be trading if a repeat purchase needs to be made. Obviously the level of concern will depend on the purchase: someone buying a stapler will not be too interested in profit levels, but a tour company ordering a cruise ship will need to make stringent checks on the financial viability of the shipbuilder as shown in its financial statements and forward projections of sales and profits.

Businesses that supply goods and services will obviously want to be confident that the business that is buying will be able to pay for the products. If the customer is a new one, the seller may well insist on a reference from the buyer's bank or may be able to obtain a financial report from an agency such as Dunn & Bradstreet.

## providers of finance

Lenders such as banks will want to be reassured that any money lent to the business will be repaid when due. They will be particularly interested in:

- profitability – can borrowing be repaid in the future?
- liquidity (the amount of money available to the business in the short term) – can that overdraft be repaid now?

## the public

The public will be interested in the financial performance of a business, either as investors looking for dividends in that business, or for political or ethical reasons – is the business making too much profit? The public is not only interested in financial information about the business, it is also interested in questions such as is it polluting the environment? Is it exploiting the labour force in developing countries? Is it experimenting on animals for research purposes? Is it involved in genetic engineering of plants used in food manufacture? As we will see, businesses such as public limited companies that publish financial information for the public are increasingly including this type of information as well.

## the tax authorities

The tax authorities will need to have financial information so that they can assess or check on how much tax will have to be paid. For example:

- VAT due to HM Customs & Excise is based on VAT charged on sales
- income tax for individuals in business (and corporation tax for limited companies) due to the Inland Revenue is based on business profit

## types of financial information available

We will now look at the types of financial information used by the stakeholders of a business in order to monitor its performance.

## financial statements

You will already have studied the main financial statements drawn up by a business. They are:

- the profit and loss account – showing sales levels and business profitability, income and expenses
- the balance sheet – showing the size of the business, how it is financed and how solvent the business is (what resources it has for repaying its debts)

Financial statements for smaller businesses are hard to come by: unlike limited company accounts, partnership and sole trader accounts are not publicly available. You may find partnerships and sole traders unwilling to release this type of information, and understandably so!

The financial statements of plc's are publicly available from the companies themselves and in abbreviated form from educational websites such as www.bized.ac.uk. The published Report and Accounts of plc's offer a interesting variety of methods of presentation of accounting information. They also provide information about issues such as environmental and social policy, which are becoming increasingly important. There are, of course other organisations which will present financial information to the public and employees: local authorities and public sector businesses, for example.

## published Annual Reports and Accounts

Public limited companies whose shares are publicly traded publish each year:

- Annual Report and Accounts – a formal report in the form of a booklet containing a profit and loss account and balance sheet (both with detailed notes) plus other information required by company law. This is sent to the shareholders unless a Summary Statement (see below) is sent instead.
- Summary Financial Statement sent to all shareholders – this is less formal and less detailed than the Report and Accounts and is intended to be easier to read and understand.

If you look at an Annual Report and Accounts you will see that it also includes a Cash Flow Statement – which is not covered by your studies. This is only required of larger companies, and sets out how money has been received and spent during a financial year. It should not under any circumstances be confused with the Cash Flow *Forecast* which is an internal budget (see Chapter 6), quite different in format, and not published with the other financial statements. Extracts from the Report & Accounts of Tesco Plc are reproduced with kind permission on pages 105 and 106.

## interpreting the financial statements

### accounting ratios

Financial statements of businesses are analysed by means of accounting ratios which indicate to the business owner and lenders how the business is performing in financial terms. The term 'accounting ratio' can be misleading because it can include percentages and straight figures as well as the normal ratio (1 : 1 for example).

The accounting ratios are normally divided into three categories:

- **solvency** – these ratios give an indication of the ability of a business to pay off its short-term debt
- **profitability** – these ratios look in a number of different ways at the profit made by a business
- **performance** – these ratios give an indication of how efficiently the business is preforming in areas such as stock holding and chasing up customer debts

### solvency

A business is solvent when it can pay its debts when they fall due.

As we have seen when looking at balance sheets a business needs cash or the ability to realise cash (eg from selling stock or being owed money by customers) as working capital. This is what the business will use to pay bills, wages, and other pressing expenses.

### who is interested in solvency?

The owner(s) of a business will want to be reassured that the business is solvent. If the owner is a sole trader or partner and the business becomes insolvent (bankrupt), their possessions may have to be sold off to pay people to whom they owe money. Lenders, too, will want to know how solvent a business is; if there are problems they will want their money back.

### measuring solvency: the current ratio

**current ratio = current assets : current liabilities**

Using figures from the balance sheet, this ratio measures the relationship between current assets and current liabilities. As we have seen, working capital (calculated as current assets minus current liabilities) is needed by all businesses in order to finance day-to-day trading activities. Sufficient working capital enables a business to hold adequate stocks, allow a measure of credit to its customers (debtors), and to pay its suppliers (creditors).

Although there is no ideal working capital ratio, an often accepted ratio is about 2:1, ie £2 of current assets to every £1 of current liabilities. However, a business in the retail trade may be able to work with a lower ratio, eg 1.5:1 or even less, because it deals mainly in sales for cash and so does not have a large figure for debtors.

The current ratio may also be expressed as a percentage:

$$\frac{\text{current assets}}{\text{current liabilities}} \times 100$$

A current ratio of 1.5 : 1 becomes 150%

## measuring solvency: acid test ratio

**acid test ratio = current assets minus stock : current liabilities**

One of the problems with the current ratio is that it includes stock in the current assets as a possible source of cash. Stock, of course, may be unsaleable or obsolete – out-of-date cans of beans, for example. The acid test ratio (also known as the quick ratio or liquid capital ratio) includes the current assets and current liabilities from the balance sheet, but stock is omitted. This is because stock is the least liquid current asset: it has to be sold first, turned into debtors, and then eventually into cash.

The balance between liquid assets, that is debtors and cash/bank, and current liabilities should, ideally, be about 1:1, ie £1 of liquid assets to each £1 of current liabilities. At this ratio a business is expected to be able to pay its current liabilities from its liquid assets; a figure below 1:1, eg 0.75:1, indicates that the business would have difficulty in meeting pressing demands from creditors. However, as with the working capital ratio, certain types of business are able to operate with a lower liquid capital ratio than others.

The acid test ratio may also be expressed as a percentage:

$$\frac{\text{current assets minus stock}}{\text{current liabilities}} \times 100$$

An acid test ratio of 1 : 1 then becomes 100%

## how are the ratios used?

With both the current and the acid test ratios, trends from one year to the next need to be considered, or comparisons made with similar organisations.

## Activity 5.1

# Solvency ratios

The following figures have been extracted from the balance sheets of Businesses A, B & C:

| Business | Total Current Assets | Stock | Current Liabilities |
|---|---|---|---|
| A | £20,000 | £5,000 | £10,000 |
| B | £20,000 | £15,000 | £10,000 |
| C | £20,000 | £15,000 | £15,000 |

1   Calculate the current and acid test ratio for all three businesses.

2   Comment on how solvent the businesses are.

3   Why would it be misleading to rely on just the current ratio for one of the businesses?

## profitability ratios

### profitability

Most people dealing with businesses will want to know how profitable they are:

- owners – because it will affect the share of profits that they will get
- managers – because they will see how close to target they are
- lenders – they will know that money is being generated to repay them
- the tax authorities – they will be able to assess the amount of tax due
- the public – they will want to know if they are getting 'value for money'
- employees – they will be reassured that their jobs are safe

### a large profit or a small profit?

Is it good policy to be seen to be making a large profit?  Generally speaking, the answer is 'yes'. There are, however, one or two exceptions. A business is taxed on its profits, and many businesses will try to bring the profit figure (and the tax bill!) down by deducting as many expenses as possible from profit.

Also, the public do not like  businesses making big profits at their expense. You may be able to think of  businesses such as BT which dominate the market and have actually reduced their prices following large profits.

## measuring profitability – gross profit percentage

You will know from your study of the profit and loss account that the gross profit of a business is the profit made after deducting from the sales figure the cost of making a product, the 'cost of sales'. The gross profit percentage is calculated using the formula:

$$\frac{\textbf{gross profit}}{\textbf{sales}} \quad \textbf{x} \quad \textbf{100} \quad = \quad \textbf{gross profit percentage}$$

This percentage relates the gross profit to sales. For example, a gross profit percentage of 50 per cent means that for every £100 of sales made, the gross profit is £50. The gross profit percentage should be similar from year-to-year for the same business. It will vary between organisations in different areas of business, eg the gross profit percentage on jewellery is considerably higher than that on baked beans. This is because jewellers sell fewer items of jewellery a week than a supermarket sells tins of baked beans.

## measuring profitability – net profit percentage

You will know from your study of the profit and loss account that the net profit of a business is the profit made after deducting all the expenses, ie the cost of sales and overheads such as insurance, advertising, business rates, fuel, and so on. The formula is:

$$\frac{\textbf{net profit}}{\textbf{sales}} \quad \textbf{x} \quad \textbf{100} \quad = \quad \textbf{net profit percentage}$$

As with gross profit percentage, the net profit percentage (or 'margin') should be similar from year-to-year for the same business, and should also be comparable with other firms in the same line of business. Any significant fall should be investigated to see if it has been caused by an increase in one particular expense, eg wages and salaries or advertising.

## measuring profitability – return on capital employed

This indicator compares the net profit of a business to the owner's capital. It gives a percentage figure which is a basic indicator of the return the owner is achieving on the capital invested in the company. The formula is:

$$\frac{\textbf{net profit}}{\textbf{owner's capital}} \quad \textbf{x} \quad \textbf{100} \quad = \quad \textbf{return on capital employed (ROCE)}$$

The owner's capital is to be found on the balance sheet in the 'Financed by' section and normally consists of capital invested plus reserves (including profit and loss) which have built up. You may find that some limited companies include long-term loans as part of capital. For the purposes of this book and external assessments you should keep to the formula quoted above.

Activity 5.2

## Profitability ratios

The following figures have been extracted from the accounts of Businesses A, B & C:

| Business | Capital Employed | Sales | Cost of sales | Other expenses |
|---|---|---|---|---|
| A | £500,000 | £500,000 | £250,000 | £200,000 |
| B | £800,000 | £800,000 | £600,000 | £160,000 |
| C | £500,000 | £600,000 | £480,000 | £100,000 |

Calculate the gross and net profit figures and then the Gross Profit Percentage, Net Profit Percentage and Return on Capital Employed, for all three businesses.

Comment on your findings, assuming that the businesses all manufacture the same type of product.

## performance ratios

We have seen that the solvency and profitability indicators are of particular interest to outside bodies. The owners and managers of a business, on the other hand, will be anxious to know how a business is performing. They are responsible for its level of performance:

*"Is the stock moving as quickly as it should?"*

*"Are our customers paying up on time?"*

*"Are we making the most efficient use of our assets?"*

There are a number of performance ratios which will provide answers to these questions.

### stock turnover

Stock turnover measures the speed with which stock 'moves' (ie is replaced because it has been sold). Clearly the more quickly it moves the better. Stock turnover can vary with the type of business. For example, a market trader selling fresh fish who finishes each day when sold out will have a stock turnover of one day. On the other hand a furniture shop may have a stock turnover of 90 days, the average length of time for which an item of furniture is held in the shop before being sold. The lower the stock turnover figure, the more efficient the organisation, for the same type of business. Stock turnover can be measured using figures from the profit and loss account:

**sales for the year** = **stock turnover (ie number of times stock is replaced)**
_____
**stock**

Some businesses measure stock turnover in days, using the formula:

**average stock x 365 days = stock turnover (in days)**
_____
**cost of sales**

The danger signs for a business are when the stock turnover period gets longer: it indicates that stock is not selling, and this in turn will hold up cash flow. Average stock is: (opening stock + closing stock) divided by 2.

## debtors' collection period

The debtors collection period shows how long, on average, debtors (ie the customers of a business) take to pay for goods sold to them on credit terms. The formula is:

**debtors x 365 days = debtors' collection period (in days)**
_____
**sales for year**

The sales figure is taken from the profit and loss account and the debtors figure from the balance sheet. The debtors collection period can be compared with that for the previous year, or with that of a similar business. In the UK, most debtors should make payment within 30 to 60 days. A comparison from year-to-year of the collection period is a measure of the business' efficiency.

## asset turnover

A business may want to know the value of sales generated from each £1 of net assets. This is calculated by the formula:

**sales (£)** = **value of sales generated by £1 of net assets**
_____
**net assets (£)**

This figure will give an indication of how efficiently the net assets are being used. Remember: net assets are total assets less external liabilities. Clearly if the figure increases from year to year, the business is becoming more efficient: each £1 of net assets is producing more sales.

It is important with this ratio that like businesses are compared with like. Some businesses, eg internet service providers, achieve high sales on low net assets, so their asset turnover figure will be high. Other businesses, eg car manufacturers have high levels of net assets; their figure will be much lower.

## Activity 5.3

# Performance ratios

The figures shown below have been extracted from the balance sheets and profit and loss accounts of a business for two years' trading. The owner is rather concerned about the situation.

Examine the figures and then answer the questions set out below.

| | Year 1 (£) | Year 2 (£) |
|---|---|---|
| **Balance sheet extract** | | |
| Net assets | 150,000 | 150,000 |
| Debtors | 12,500 | 25,000 |
| | | |
| **Profit and loss account extract** | | |
| Sales | 100,000 | 95,000 |
| Purchases | 50,000 | 60,000 |
| Opening stock | 15,000 | 17,500 |
| Closing stock | 17,500 | 30,000 |
| Cost of sales | 47,500 | 47,500 |
| Overheads | 22,000 | 25,000 |

1     Calculate the following performance indicators for both years of trading:

    (a)   stock turnover (days) – assume average stock for Year 1 is the closing stock

    (b)   debtor collection period (days)

    (c)   asset turnover (£)

2     Comment on the significance of the figures you have produced (do not just say they have 'gone up' or 'gone down'). Identify any problems you can see and suggest possible solutions.

## the use of accounting ratios

It is important to appreciate that accounting ratios should not be listed in a mechanical way but should be used for a purpose. They should be analysed and presented in a meaningful way to people in the business such as owners and managers or people outside the business.

The process of financial analysis is like a doctor examining a patient: it is a a process of observation, measurement (pulse, temperature and blood pressure), combined with experience and judgement.

### shortcomings of accounting ratios

Accounting ratios do have shortcomings: they are not the complete answer to financial analysis. These shortcomings include:

- they only look back at financial statements in the past; they may not be valid for forward projections

- inflation can affect the figures: a small percentage increase in sales, for example, may be a fall in real terms

- an over-reliance on formulas can be misleading, eg saying that any current ratio less than 1.5 : 1 shows a weakness in working capital

In the Case Study which follows we will take two years' figures from Classy Foods Limited, a manufacturer of quality cakes, and interpret them for the benefit of the bank that is being asked to lend money.

## Case Study

# Classy Foods Limited
# using accounting ratios

Classy Foods Limited makes cakes and pastries for the catering trade. The company needs to raise a £50,000 bank loan to finance the expansion of its premises and the purchase of freezers for its perishable products. The management have called in an accountant to help them draft a business plan.

The management needs to convince the bank that the business is flourishing, and they will achieve this by presenting the bank with a business plan containing the last two years' financial statements and key accounting ratios . . .

---

**CLASSY FOODS LIMITED**

**SUMMARY PROFIT AND loss accounts**

|  | £ | £ |
|---|---|---|
|  | Year 20-1 | Year 20-2 |
| Purchases (all on credit) | 72,000 | 95,000 |
| Sales (all on credit) | 225,000 | 278,000 |
| Cost of Sales | 70,000 | 93,000 |
| GROSS PROFIT | 155,000 | 185,000 |
| NET PROFIT | 45,000 | 68,000 |

**CLASSY FOODS LIMITED**
**BALANCE SHEETS**

| | £ | £ |
|---|---|---|
| | 31 Dec 20-1 | 31 Dec 20-2 |
| FIXED ASSETS | 205,500 | 265,700 |
| CURRENT ASSETS | | |
| Stock | 3,500 | 5,500 |
| Debtors | 30,000 | 31,300 |
| | 33,500 | 36,800 |
| CURRENT LIABILITIES | | |
| Creditors | 10,000 | 12,000 |
| Bank Overdraft | 14,000 | 10,000 |
| | 24,000 | 22,000 |
| WORKING CAPITAL | 9,500 | 14,800 |
| | 215,000 | 280,500 |
| LESS LONG-TERM LIABILITIES | | |
| Long-term loan | 35,000 | 32,500 |
| **NET ASSETS** | 180,000 | 248,000 |
| | | |
| **FINANCED BY** | | |
| AUTHORISED AND ISSUED SHARE CAPITAL | | |
| 100,000 shares £1 each fully paid | 100,000 | 100,000 |
| Reserves | 80,000 | 148,000 |
| SHAREHOLDERS' FUNDS | 180,000 | 248,000 |

**CLASSY FOODS LIMITED**

**KEY ACCOUNTING RATIOS FOR THE YEARS 20-1 AND 20-2**

| **solvency** | 20-1 | 20-2 |
|---|---|---|
| Current Ratio | 1.40 : 1 | 1.67 : 1 |
| Acid Test Ratio | 1.25 : 1 | 1.42 : 1 |

| **profitability** | 20-1 | 20-2 |
|---|---|---|
| Gross Profit Percentage | 69% | 67% |
| Net Profit Percentage | 20% | 24% |
| Return on Capital Employed | 21% | 24% |

| **performance** | 20-1 | 20-2 |
|---|---|---|
| Stock Turnover Period | 18 days | 18 days |
| Debtor Collection Period | 49 days | 41 days |
| Asset Turnover | £1.25 per £1 | £1.12 per £1 |

## comments on financial performance

The accountant is likely to make the comments along the lines of the following to the management of the company:

## solvency

This business, which deals with perishable goods, keeps a low stock level, which reduces the liquidity ratios of the company. The current ratio increased from 1.40 : 1 to 1.67 : 1, indicating a rise in working capital to a very acceptable level, taking into consideration the low stock holding, and the guideline 2 : 1 ratio.

The acid test ratio, which excludes stock, is therefore of less significance for this company. It has increased over the year from 1.25 : 1 to a comfortable 1.42 : 1. Both figures are better than the guideline of 1 : 1.

## profitability

Sales have increased by 24% over the year, which is encouraging.

Gross profit percentage remains steady, the slight drop of 2% probably representing a rise in raw material costs, notably dairy products.

Net profit percentage increased by 4% to 24%, reflecting increased efficiency and trimming of overhead expenses.

Return on capital employed rose from 21% to 24%, showing a healthy return on capital invested.

## performance

Stock turnover period has remained unchanged at 18 days, a high figure, as would be expected with a company dealing with perishable goods. If the company did not have the freezers in which it keeps some of its stock, the figure would be even higher.

The debtor collection period has shortened from 49 to 41 days, improving the cash flow of the company.

Asset turnover has reduced slightly from £1.25 of sales per £1 of Net Assets to £1.12 of sales per £1 of Net Assets. The reason for this is not that sales have declined (they have gone up by 24% over the year) but because Net Assets have increased by 38%, reflecting the healthy net profit made during the year (net profit is added into the Reserves).

The bank, which has staff skilled in the interpretation of financial statements, will undoubtedly come to the same conclusion. They will be happy to lend the company the money it needs, as long as its Cash Flow Forecast shows that it can afford the repayments.

## Activity 5.4

# Interpreting the accounts

You are a clerk at the Greenham branch of the National Bank plc. Your present job involves assessing lending applications from your customers and writing analytical notes for your manager, Lionel Stirling. This process of financial analysis requires you to examine sets of final accounts and to extract relevant accounting ratios. During the course of a day's work you are requested to undertake a number of tasks.

### Task One: Becker Packaging Limited

Becker Packaging Limited is the holding company of a group of companies whose account you hold at the bank. It owns two subsidiary companies, Cardbox Limited and Easywrap Limited. You have recently received the final accounts of these two companies.

You are to extract relevant accounting ratios for both companies and set them out in a table for comparison purposes. Write notes covering profitability, solvency and performance for the guidance of Mr Stirling. You are given the following extracts from trading and profit and loss accounts for the year ended 31 March 20-4 and the balance sheets as at that date:

|  | Cardbox Ltd | Easywrap Ltd |
| --- | --- | --- |
|  | £ | £ |
| Sales | 175,000 | 200,000 |
| Cost of sales | 120,000 | 150,000 |
| Gross profit | 55,000 | 50,000 |
| Net profit | 25,000 | 35,000 |
| Fixed assets | 100,000 | 120,000 |
| Stock | 45,000 | 50,000 |
| Debtors | 17,500 | 25,000 |
| Creditors | 15,000 | 21,500 |
| Bank overdraft | 9,200 | 8,500 |
| Share capital and reserves | 118,300 | 130,000 |
| Long term loan | 20,000 | 35,000 |

Assume for your calculations that all sales are credit sales and the closing stock figure is an average for the year.

## Task Two: Connors Sportsware Limited

Connors Sportsware Limited is a good customer of your bank and has recently been given a long term loan of £20,000 to refit and expand the business premises. The directors have recently approached your bank with a request for an overdraft of £10,000 for new stock. The cash flow forecast shows that the company can repay this amount over six months, after which time the situation can be reviewed. Mr Stirling hands you the final accounts for the last two years and asks you to work out ratios to show if the company is as sound as he thinks it is.

You are to work out relevant ratios for the two years and then write notes comparing the two years in respect of profitability, solvency, and performance for the guidance of Mr Stirling.

Extracts from trading and profit and loss accounts for the years ended 30 June 20-3 and 20-4, and the balance sheets at that date:

|  | 20-3 £ | 20-4 £ |
|---|---|---|
| Sales | 240,000 | 400,000 |
| Cost of sales | 160,000 | 300,000 |
| Purchases | 160,000 | 318,000 |
| Gross profit | 80,000 | 100,000 |
| Net profit | 60,000 | 70,000 |
|  |  |  |
| Fixed assets | 70,000 | 75,000 |
| Stock | 14,000 | 32,000 |
| Debtors | 24,000 | 40,000 |
| Bank | 2,000 | 3,000 |
| Creditors | 20,000 | 40,000 |
| Share capital and reserves | 70,000 | 90,000 |
| Long term loan | 20,000 | 20,000 |

Assume for your calculations that all sales are credit sales, and average stock for 20-3 is closing stock.

### Task Three: MacInrays Mints Limited

MacInrays Mints Limited manufactures confectionery. The Finance Director, John MacInray has recently approached Mr Stirling to ask for a overdraft of £25,000 for expansion of trading. John MacInray has brought in the latest set of accounts for the year ended 30 June 20-4, and Mr Stirling has asked you to analyse them.

You are to extract accounting ratios and write comments for Mr Stirling on the financial strength or otherwise of the company.

|  | £ |
|---|---|
| Sales | 175,000 |
| Cost of sales | 145,000 |
| Gross profit | 30,000 |
| Net profit | 1,500 |
|  |  |
| Fixed assets | 25,000 |
| Stock | 70,000 |
| Debtors | 10,000 |
| Creditors | 65,000 |
| Bank overdraft | 12,000 |
| Share capital and reserves | 13,000 |
| Medium term loan | 15,000 |

Assume for your calculations that all sales are credit sales and that the closing stock figure is an average for the year.

## performance of public limited companies

The number of people investing their money in public limited companies has increased significantly in recent years, particularly since investors have been able to buy and sell shares on the internet. Investors in public limited companies will be interested in a number of financial indicators.

### financial indicators of shares

The price paid for a share in a 'quoted' company traded on the stock markets will vary from day to day. If there is confidence in that company and confidence in the stock market as a whole, the price should go up over time. If the company is not doing so well (for instance if its profits go down) or if investors lose confidence in the stock market, the price is likely to go down.

The movement of prices in the stock market is tracked by a variety of different indices, including the FTSE 100 index and the FTSE Allshare index. These relate the level of share prices to a numerical base.

## how to profit from investing in shares

Investors hope to make money from two sources:

- a rise in the price of the shares held – the idea is to 'buy low, sell high'
- the dividends paid by the company each year - the 'yield' of the shares

There are many different sources of information about share prices and dividends paid, including the financial pages of the press and financial data on the internet (eg Yahoo stock price pages). The financial pages of a newspaper such as The Times will show share prices and yields like this.

| High | Low | Company | Price (p) | +/– | Yield | Price/ Earnings |
|------|-----|---------|-----------|-----|-------|-----------------|
| 304 | 160 | Safeway | 200 | + 2 | 6.3 | 9.3 |
| 480 | 286 | Sainsbury J | 340 | + 10 | 4.2 | 24.4 |
| 201 | 152 | Tesco | 162 | + 11 | 2.6 | 18.3 |

These need some explanation:

### high/low

These are the highest and lowest price of the share over the last twelve months. As you can see from the figures shown above, the variation (and the potential to make money) is substantial.

### company

The name of the public limited company. Companies are normally classified into sectors according to what they do. The companies here are all in the 'Retailers and Food' sector.

### price

If you look in a newspaper this is the price in pence of the share the previous day. If you access the internet or teletext you can get same day prices.

### +/–

This is the rise or fall in the price of the share over the previous day. The rise or fall is quoted in pence.

## yield

This is short for 'dividend yield'. The dividend is the payment made to shareholders, normally out of the profits of a company. It relates the dividend to the market price of the share and is quoted as a percentage. It basically says how many pence you are likely to get per £1 invested. The higher the figure, the more money the investor will receive. The formula is:

$$\frac{\text{share dividend (in pence)}}{\text{market price of share}} \times 100 = \text{dividend yield}$$

## price/earnings

The 'earnings' of a share is the amount of profit made by a company for every share issued. This is not the same as the dividend because not all profits are paid out in dividends. Companies keep and invest ('retain') a proportion of profits. The price/earnings ratio links the market price of the share and the profitability of the company. The formula is:

$$\frac{\text{market price of share (in pence)}}{\text{earnings per share (in pence)}} = \text{price/earnings ratio}$$

The higher the ratio the more 'expensive' the share is seen to be.

## Activity 5.5

# Who wants to be a millionaire?

This Activity will enable each student to choose and invest in shares on a competitive basis, and hopefully see a gain in 'capital' value. Each member of the class has £10,000 to invest over a time period, for example a term. The tasks listed below are a guideline only and may be varied by the teacher/lecturer to suit the situation.

1  Each student should invest a notional £10,000 in the shares of three companies chosen from the pages of the financial press or on-line financial sites.

2  The number of shares purchased, their price and reasons for the choice should be written down. Reference should be made to investor indicators such as dividend yield, price/earnings ratio, current pricing in the market and any articles and 'tips' in the press or on financial sites and bulletin boards on the internet

3  The written records should be given to the teacher/lecturer to keep in a file.

4  While the shares are held students should look out for articles about the companies in the press, or on the individual company websites and add them to their pages in the file.

5  At the end of the period each student should calculate the total value of the shares, and write a short summary, pointing out the reasons for the success or failure of their investments. They should then between them draw up a class league table.

# financial information in published accounts

Public limited companies whose shares are traded on the stock markets publish each year an Annual Report and Accounts. This is a formal report in the form of a booklet containing the financial statements and other financial details required by law. Traded public limited companies also publish an Annual Summary which is sent to all shareholders; this is a less formal, less detailed and more 'glossy' document than the Report and Accounts and is intended to be easier to read and more suitable for investors.

As part of your studies you should obtain both the formal Annual Report and Accounts and the Annual Summary of the public limited companies you are investigating. Your external assessment may contain extracts from these types of document and you should be familiar with them and prepared to answer questions on the figures they contain.

Shown below are extracts from the Annual Summary of Tesco Plc. Study them and carry out the Activity on page 107.

| Profit and loss account | 1999 52 weeks £m | 1998* 52 weeks (proforma) £m | 1998 53 weeks (restated) £m |
|---|---|---|---|
| **Sales at net selling price** | **18,546** | 17,447 | 17,779 |
| **Turnover excluding value added tax** | **17,158** | 16,142 | 16,452 |
| Operating expenses | **(16,155)** | (15,212) | (15,505) |
| Employee profit-sharing | **(38)** | (35) | (35) |
| **Operating profit** | **965** | 895 | 912 |
| Profit/(loss) from joint ventures | **6** | (6) | (6) |
| Interest | **(90)** | (72) | (74) |
| **Underlying pre-tax profit** | **881** | 817 | 832 |
| Loss on disposal of fixed assets/operations | **(8)** | (9) | (9) |
| Integration costs | **(26)** | (63) | (63) |
| Goodwill amortisation | **(5)** | – | – |
| **Profit before tax** | **842** | 745 | 760 |
| Tax | **(237)** | (223) | (228) |
| Minority interest | **1** | – | – |
| **Profit for the financial year** | **606** | 522 | 532 |
| Dividends | **(277)** | (255) | (255) |
| **Retained profit** | **329** | 267 | 277 |
| **Adjusted diluted earnings per share** [†] | **9.37p** | 8.70p | 8.84p |
| **Dividend per share** | **4.12p** | 3.87p | 3.87p |

[†] Excluding goodwill amortisation, integration costs, net losses on disposal of fixed assets and discontinued operations.
\* 1998/99 was a 52 week year compared to 53 weeks for 1997/98. A proforma 52 week profit and loss account for 1998 has been used for comparison.

Profit and loss account from the Tesco Plc Annual Summary

## Balance sheet

| | 1999 £m | 1998 (restated) £m |
|---|---|---|
| **Fixed assets** | 7,553 | 6,496 |
| Current assets | 1,146 | 942 |
| Short term creditors | (3,075) | (2,713) |
| **Net current liabilities** | (1,929) | (1,771) |
| **Total assets less current liabilities** | 5,624 | 4,725 |
| Long term creditors | (1,230) | (812) |
| Provisions | (17) | (10) |
| **Total net assets** | 4,377 | 3,903 |

**Terry Leahy**
**Andrew Higginson**
Directors

The summary financial statement was approved by the Board on 12 April 1999.

Balance sheet from the Tesco Plc Annual Summary

**extract from Chairman's statement**

"We have made good progress with our strategy of growing the UK business and developing the foundations for additional future growth from international markets"

# investor information

## summary five year record

| Year ended February | 1995 £m | 1996 £m | 1997 £m | 1998 52 weeks (proforma) £m | 1999 £m |
|---|---|---|---|---|---|
| **Turnover excluding VAT** | | | | | |
| UK | 9,655 | 11,560 | 13,118 | 14,677 | 15,835 |
| Rest of Europe | 446 | 534 | 769 | 1,465 | 1,167 |
| Thailand | – | – | – | – | 156 |
| | 10,101 | 12,094 | 13,887 | 16,142 | 17,158 |
| **Operating profit** (pre-integration costs and goodwill amortisation) | | | | | |
| UK | 600 | 713 | 760 | 859 | 919 |
| Rest of Europe | 17 | 11 | 14 | 36 | 48 |
| Thailand | – | – | – | – | (2) |
| | 617 | 724 | 774 | 895 | 965 |
| **Underlying profit** | 595 | 681 | 750 | 817 | 881 |
| **Profit before tax** | 551 | 675 | 750 | 745 | 842 |
| **Adjusted diluted earnings per share** | 6.70p | 7.30p | 7.83p | 8.70p | 9.37p |
| **Dividend per share** | 2.87p | 3.20p | 3.45p | 3.87p | 4.12p |
| **UK food retailing productivity** | | | | | |
| Turnover per employee (£) | 140,842 | 143,335 | 146,326 | 139,770 | 146,236 |
| Weekly sales per sq ft (£) | 17.00 | 18.31 | 19.74 | 20.48 | 21.05 |
| **UK food retail statistics** | | | | | |
| Market share in food and drink shops | 12.0% | 13.7% | 14.6% | 15.2% | 15.8% |
| Number of stores | 519 | 545 | 568 | 618 | 639 |
| Total sales area (000 sq ft) | 12,641 | 13,397 | 14,036 | 15,215 | 15,975 |
| Full-time equivalent employees | 68,552 | 80,650 | 89,649 | 105,008 | 108,284 |

Investor information from the Tesco Plc Annual Summary

## Activity 5.6

# Interpreting published accounts
# Tesco PLC

Study the financial information from Tesco's Annual Summary shown on the previous two pages. Note that:

- money amounts are quoted in £millions
- minus figures are shown in brackets

**Answer the following questions**

1   What is the percentage increase in total Turnover (sales) over the five years?

Produce a line graph or bar chart showing the trend. If possible, using a charting facility on your computer to do this (most spreadsheets provide this function).

Comment on the trend shown.

2   What is the percentage increase in Profit before Tax over the same period?

How does this trend affect the amount of money paid to shareholders in the form of dividends?

3   Comment on the earnings per share shown in the Profit and Loss account.

Is this indicator the same as the price/earnings ratio? If not, how is it different?

4   What is the main aim of Tesco PLC? Why do you think the company has adopted this policy?

What evidence can you see from the figures shown in these statements that this aim has been successful in recent years?

5   Many of the figures in the Profit and Loss Account represent the interests of various stakeholders in the company.

Identify these stakeholders and explain what figures in particular will apply to them.

6   Comment on the working capital (net current liabilities) of the business as it is shown on the balance sheet.

Is there a problem here?

What does this tell you about the interpretation of accounting ratios?

## CHAPTER SUMMARY

● Many different stakeholders have an interest in the financial performance of a business; they include:

- owners, managers and employees

- customers and suppliers

- lenders

- investors

- the public

- regulatory bodies

● The main documents for providing financial information to stakeholders are the profit and loss account and the balance sheet.

● Public limited companies publish their financial statements in two forms: the detailed Report and Accounts (as required by law) and a summarised version known as a Summary Financial Statement or Annual Review produced mainly for investors in the company.

● Accounting ratios can be extracted from the financial statements to provide stakeholders with indicators of the financial 'health' of a business.

● Solvency ratios measure the ability of a business to repay its debts. They analyse the working capital position on the balance sheet; they include the current ratio and the acid test ratio.

● Profitability ratios analyse the relationship of various measures of profit against figures including sales (gross profit percentage and net profit percentage) and owner's capital (return on capital employed).

● Performance ratios are useful for managers. They examine areas such as the length of time for which stock is held (stock turnover), the period of time customers take to pay their bills (debtor collection period) and the amount of sales generated from assets (asset turnover).

● Accounting ratios should be treated with a certain amount of caution: they only look back over past financial periods, they can be affected by inflation and they need to be interpreted carefully according to the type of business involved.

● Investors in public limited companies whose shares are traded on the stock markets are able to assess the company on a number of different financial indicators including:

- the share price as it fluctuates over time

- dividend yield as it relates to the market price of the shares

- price/earnings ratio which relates profit to market price

## KEY TERMS

| | |
|---|---|
| **profit and loss account** | a financial statement which measures the profit made by a business over a financial period |
| **balance sheet** | a financial statement which shows at any one time how a business is financed, its working capital position and the owner's capital |
| **cash flow statement** | a financial statement which measures the flow of money in and out of a business over a financial period (not assessed in this unit) |
| **accounting ratio** | a financial indicator, which can be a ratio, a percentage or a time period, extracted from the financial statements of a business to provide stakeholders with a means of assessing its financial state |
| **current ratio** | current assets : current liabilities |
| **acid test ratio** | current assets minus stock : current liabilities |
| **gross profit %** | $\dfrac{\text{gross profit} \times 100}{\text{sales}}$ |
| **net profit %** | $\dfrac{\text{net profit} \times 100}{\text{sales}}$ |
| **return on capital employed** | $\dfrac{\text{net profit} \times 100}{\text{owners capital}}$ |
| **stock turnover (days)** | $\dfrac{\text{average stock} \times 365 \text{ days}}{\text{cost of sales}}$ |
| **debtors collection period** | $\dfrac{\text{debtors} \times 365 \text{ days}}{\text{sales for year}}$ |
| **asset turnover** | $\dfrac{\text{sales (£)}}{\text{net assets (£)}}$ |
| **share price** | the price (in pence) of a traded share |
| **dividend yield** | $\dfrac{\text{share dividend (in pence)}}{\text{market price of share (in pence)}} \times 100$ |
| **price/earnings ratio** | $\dfrac{\text{market price of share (in pence)}}{\text{earnings (ie profit earned) per share (in pence)}}$ |

# 6

# Budgeting in business

## introduction

The management of a business needs to plan for the future, both for the short term and for the long term. Short-term plans involve the drawing up of budgets which set annual targets for different functions within the business. As the year passes the budget targets are compared with the actual figures and discrepancies are picked up and action is taken as appropriate. Budgets therefore help management to keep its 'fingers on the pulse' of the business and thereby control it.

## what you will learn from this chapter

- business planning can be long-term (the five year 'corporate plan') or short-term (the one year 'operational plan')

- an important part of the business planning process is the setting of budgets which help management to measure performance and to make decisions

- budgets can be function budgets (which set targets for functional areas within the business), and departmental budgets (which cover the performance of individual departments)

- the individual budgets combine into the cash budget (which forecasts the flow of money in and out of the business bank account) and the master budget (which sets out a forecast profit and loss account and a forecast balance sheet)

- budgets can be income budgets (eg sales budget) or expenditure budgets (eg staffing budget); they are normally expressed in money terms, but can be expressed in units (eg production budget)

- during the course of the year the budget projections will be compared with the actual figures and any difference ('variance') will be reported and acted upon

# introduction to business planning

## business planning and business plans

What is business planning? It is an ongoing process involving the setting of objectives and the monitoring of progress. It is important not to confuse the business planning process with the 'business plan' document you will encounter if you study Unit 6 'Business Planning'. This 'business plan' is a formal written document compiled normally when a business wants to raise finance. It is presented to a lender or major investor and sets out in a persuasive way why lending to the business (or investing in the business) is a feasible proposition. The business plan is the way a business 'sells itself' to a provider of finance, such as a bank.

## the planning and monitoring cycle

Businesses should constantly be planning ahead. They may be planning specific projects, or they may be looking at the year ahead in order to calculate staffing and estimate sales. Whatever the situation, there are four distinct stages in the planning process:

1  set objectives – for example to increase sales by 25%

2  collect information – assess the situation – can the business produce 25% more goods? how much will it cost? can it sell them?

3  make specific plans – expand production, take on more staff

4  see how the business is getting on – the business can look at its sales figures each month, see if it is achieving its target, and try to do something about it if it is not

Now see how these four stages form the planning cycle shown in the diagram below. As we will see later, they all involve budgeting.

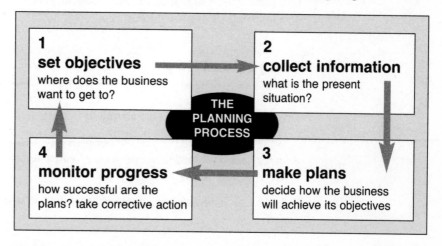

1 **set objectives**
where does the business want to get to?

2 **collect information**
what is the present situation?

THE PLANNING PROCESS

4 **monitor progress**
how successful are the plans? take corrective action

3 **make plans**
decide how the business will achieve its objectives

## types of plans

Planning by a business can be divided into three distinct areas:

### mission statement and vision statement

A mission statement is a public statement by the business setting out in general terms what the business does, what it aims to achieve, its values and standards. A vision statement is a more general statement of how the business sees itself developing in the future – a 'vision' of what it wants to be.

### corporate plan

This contains the long-term objectives of the business (up to five years, for example) and involves all areas of business activity, eg profitability, market share, product range, staffing, environmental policy. The Corporate Plan is the responsibility of the highest levels of management of the business.

### operational plans and budgets

The operational planning process follows the setting of objectives, ie the Corporate Plan and the gathering of internal and external information. Operational plans are normally for one year in functional areas such as sales, marketing, production, finance, human resources and administration. Operational plans set out the detail dictated by the objectives of the business, eg the number of products produced, pay rates, the amount of finance to be raised, the introduction of new technology. These plans will set specific targets for the business – and will require budgets (see below).

Operational plans are normally set by individual departments within the business – eg sales and marketing, production, finance – and will be the responsibility of the departmental manager. Operational plans are normally set for one financial year at a time. Plans are constantly reviewed and monitored by the people responsible for them. Towards the end of each year, new plans will be drawn up for the following year, taking into account all the developments during the current year.

## budget setting

Operational plans involve the setting of budgets by departments and also by function. What exactly is a budget?

*A budget is a table setting out projected figures for specific areas of business activity such as sales and production.*

*A budget is a method of planning, monitoring and controlling business activity.*

A budget is based on information – past and current – and forecasts. It covers a set period of time, normally a year.  A budget can deal with:

- income – eg from sales
- expenditure – eg production, staffing

A budget is commonly set in financial terms, eg a sales revenue budget, but it can also be expressed in terms of units, eg items produced, workers employed, items sold.

## timescale of budgets

Most budgets are prepared for the financial year, and are usually broken down into shorter time periods, usually monthly.  As time passes the actual figures achieved by the business can be compared with the budgeted figures and the differences between the two – the 'variances' – can be entered on a report and investigated if necessary.

## benefits of budgets

Budgets provide benefits both for the business and also for its managers:

### assisting decision making

Budgets help the management of businesses to see the outcome of different courses of action and to make decisions accordingly.

### motivating staff

Budgets motivate staff by setting targets which have to be met.  This can, of course, only take place if the targets are realistic!

### measuring performance

Budgets enable businesses to see how successful they are in meeting targets, eg sales, production, staff costs.

## types of budget

There are two main types of budget: the function budget and the departmental budget.

### function budget

The function budget is a plan for a specific function within a business, eg:

- sales budget – which covers sales income to be received by the business
- production budget – which covers the number and cost of items produced
- staffing budget – which plans the workforce's wages and salaries costs

### departmental budget

The costs of running a business set out in the function budgets are also included by its operating departments in departmental budgets, eg sales department budget, administration department budget. The object here is to make each department run efficiently: its managers – known as the budget holders – will be set specific targets for spending and productivity in terms of staffing and spending, for example.

### the master budget

The end result of the budgeting process is the production of a cash budget and a master budget which takes the form of forecast financial statements – an estimated profit and loss account and balance sheet at the end of the budget period. The master budget is the 'master plan' which shows how all the budgets 'work together'. Look at the diagram on the next page, which shows how all the budgets are related to each other.

### limiting factors

A limiting factor is an aspect of the business which prevents it from expanding its operations any further – for example the volume of its products that it can sell. Other limiting factors include the availability of raw materials, skilled labour, factory and office space, or finance.

It is essential to identify these limiting factors. For most businesses the main limiting factor is sales – how much of its product range can a business sell? The starting point for the budgeting process is therefore normally the sales budget. The order in which the budgets are drafted will often be:

- **sales budget** – what can the business sell in the next twelve months?
- **production budget** – how can the business make all the items which it plans to sell?
- **staffing**, **purchases** and **overheads budgets** – what resources in terms of labour and raw materials will the business need to produce the items? – what other expenses will be incurred?
- **departmental budgets** – what resources will be needed by individual departments?
- **capital budget** – what fixed assets (eg machinery, vehicles) need to be purchased over the next twelve months?
- **cash budget** – what money will be flowing in and out of the bank account?
- **master budget** – a summary of all the budgets to provide projected financial statements, ie a profit and loss account and balance sheet

Study the diagram on the next page. It shows this process in action . . .

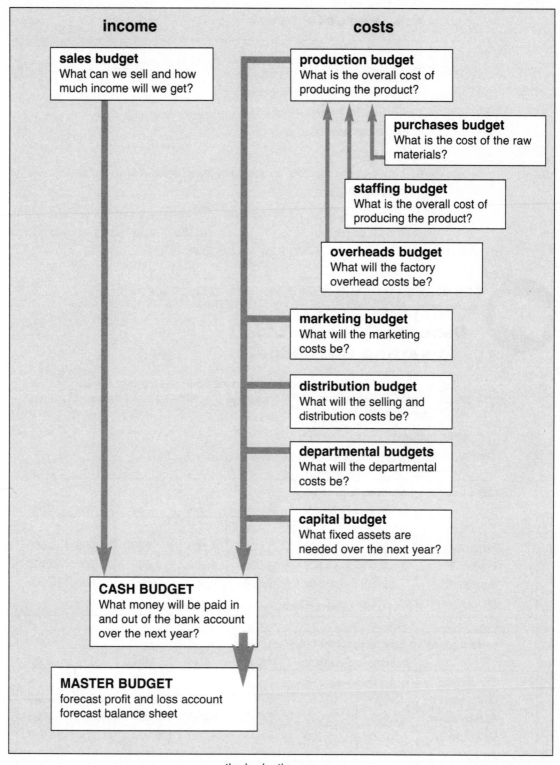

**income**

**sales budget**
What can we sell and how much income will we get?

**costs**

**production budget**
What is the overall cost of producing the product?

**purchases budget**
What is the cost of the raw materials?

**staffing budget**
What is the overall cost of producing the product?

**overheads budget**
What will the factory overhead costs be?

**marketing budget**
What will the marketing costs be?

**distribution budget**
What will the selling and distribution costs be?

**departmental budgets**
What will the departmental costs be?

**capital budget**
What fixed assets are needed over the next year?

**CASH BUDGET**
What money will be paid in and out of the bank account over the next year?

**MASTER BUDGET**
forecast profit and loss account
forecast balance sheet

the budgeting process

## how budgets 'work'

This Unit does not require you to construct all the different types of budget 'from scratch', but rather to appreciate:

- the different types of budget
- what they are for
- how they work
- how they 'fit together' in the planning process – as in the diagram on the previous page

The Cash Budget is one of the most important types of budget and will be dealt with on pages 123 to 131. The Case Study below sets out examples of some of the most common types of budget.

### Case Study

# Osborne Giftware Ltd
## setting the budgets

Osborne Giftware Limited imports novelty goods and sells them in the UK through shops, agency sales and mail order. It also manufactures a limited number of games in its factory near Bolton.

### sales budgets

Set out below are two of its sales budgets for the coming year.

| sales budget by product (extract) | | | | | | | |
|---|---|---|---|---|---|---|---|
| | January | February | March | April | May | June | Total |
| | £ | £ | £ | £ | £ | £ | £ |
| Product A | 1,000 | 1,000 | 1,000 | 1,000 | 1,000 | 1,000 | 6,000 |
| Product B | 1,500 | 1,500 | 1,500 | 1,500 | 1,500 | 1,500 | 9,000 |
| Product C | 2,500 | 2,500 | 2,500 | 2,500 | 2,500 | 2,500 | 15,000 |
| etc . . . | | | | | | | |

| sales budget by type of customer (extract) | | | | | | | |
|---|---|---|---|---|---|---|---|
| | January | February | March | April | May | June | Total |
| | £ | £ | £ | £ | £ | £ | £ |
| Direct sales | 10,000 | 10,000 | 10,000 | 12,000 | 12,000 | 12,000 | 66,000 |
| Agency sales | 5,000 | 5,000 | 5,000 | 5,000 | 5,000 | 5,000 | 30,000 |
| Mail order | 5,000 | 5,000 | 6,000 | 5,000 | 6,000 | 6,000 | 33,000 |
| etc . . . | | | | | | | |

Certain aspects of the structure of the sales budget (and any budget) will stay constant, whether they are income budgets or expenditure budgets. For example, the budget is subdivided into 'budget periods': either months or four-weekly periods (the 52 week year is conveniently divided into 13 four-weekly periods). The extracts from the sales budgets on the previous page show six of the usual twelve monthly periods.

## production budget

When Osborne Giftware has established its sales budget ('How many of each product can we sell?') it is then in a position to work out its production budget for the items it manufactures ('How can we make those products on time?'). It must be stressed that a production budget applies to a manufacturing business; a business providing a service will carry out a similar process using an 'operating budget.'

The production budget will take into account when in the year the manufactured items (games) will be needed and when they are likely to be sold. The budget therefore shows:
* the projected monthly sales figures
* the finished products in stock at the beginning and end of each month

### production budget

| UNITS | Jan | Feb | Mar | Apr | May | Jun | Jul | Aug | Sep | Oct | Nov | Dec |
|---|---|---|---|---|---|---|---|---|---|---|---|---|
| Opening stock | 100 | 275 | 450 | 600 | 550 | 500 | 450 | 300 | 175 | 325 | 475 | 125 |
| add Units produced | 325 | 325 | 350 | 350 | 350 | 350 | 350 | 175 | 350 | 350 | 350 | 400 |
| less Units sold | 150 | 150 | 200 | 400 | 400 | 400 | 500 | 300 | 200 | 200 | 700 | 425 |
| Closing stock | 275 | 450 | 600 | 550 | 500 | 450 | 300 | 175 | 325 | 475 | 125 | 100 |

You will see from the production budget that it shows units of production. When the monthly production of units has been calculated, the budget can then be expressed in money terms – it will become a production cost budget  This will be made possible by applying a standard cost worked out by the business from the raw materials cost, the labour cost and the overheads (other expenses) which were needed to manufacture a single unit of production.

## staffing budget

The staffing budget is a function budget which covers the staffing costs of all the departments within the business. It includes the pay before deductions, the employer's National Insurance and pension contributions. Six months' figures are shown here.

### staffing budget (extract)

| | January £ | February £ | March £ | April £ | May £ | June £ |
|---|---|---|---|---|---|---|
| Gross pay | 40,000 | 40,000 | 40,000 | 40,000 | 40,000 | 40,000 |
| National Insurance | 4,080 | 4,080 | 4,080 | 4,080 | 4,080 | 4,080 |
| Pension payments | 2,000 | 2,000 | 2,000 | 2,000 | 2,000 | 2,000 |

## budget reports – variances

The budget, once it is set for the financial year, is monitored by comparing actual results with the targeted figures. Any differences between the two are known as **variances**.

budgeted figures – actual figures  =  variances

Departmental managers in a business (in charge of 'budget centres') will base their decisions on departmental **budget reports**, normally produced by the finance department. Less significant variances will be dealt with by the manager and his supervisors; significant variances will need to be referred to a higher management level. Many variances, if they are very small, will not need acting on at all.

The illustration below sets out the format of a typical budget report for a sales department. The details shown are:

- the budget centre (sales department) and the budget holder responsible (the manager)
- budget, actual and variance figures for the current period (October here)
- year-to-date figures (these are optional)
- the variance trends:  'FAV' is short for 'favourable', ie better than budget, 'ADV' is short for 'adverse', ie worse than budget
- comments – the column here would be enough to record the reasons for smaller variances, but the manager would expect to receive a more detailed report for significant variances

## BUDGET REPORT

**Budget Centre**  Sales Department          **Budget Holder**  T Hussain

**Period**  October 2001                      **Date**  7 November 2001

|  | current period | | | | year-to-date | | | | comments |
|---|---|---|---|---|---|---|---|---|---|
|  | budget £000 | actual £000 | variance £000 | trend | budget £000 | actual £000 | variance £000 | trend |  |
| Product A | 200 | 250 | + 50 | FAV | 2,750 | 3,125 | + 375 | FAV |  |
| Product B | 225 | 200 | - 25 | ADV | 1,275 | 1,150 | - 125 | ADV |  |
| Product C | 425 | 450 | + 25 | FAV | 4,025 | 4,475 | + 450 | FAV |  |

# factors that cause variances

You may be asked in your assessment to:

- identify different types of variance
- comment on the factors that cause those variances

## sales variance

**sales variance = actual sales minus budgeted sales**

A **favourable** (positive) variance will result when sales are better than budgeted. This might be the result of the price going up when demand for the product is strong, or special promotional offers for the product.

An **adverse** (negative) variance will result when sales are worse than budgeted. A *fall* in sales income from a particular product might be the result of overpricing or ineffective marketing.

Whatever the cause, if the variance is significant, management will need to take action. If sales are better than budget, management will make sure the success is continued through pushing up production and ensuring the marketing effort is continued. If sales are down, management will want to know why. Is the price right? Can marketing be improved? Is the product going out of fashion? Should the business be switching to other products?

The sales variance relates to **income**. Materials, labour and overhead variances, on the other hand, relate to **expenses**.

## materials variance

**materials variance = standard (budgeted) cost of materials minus actual cost**

Note here that the budgeted cost is referred to as the 'standard cost'. This is the cost of the quantity of materials a manufacturing business expects to use.

A **favourable** (positive) variance will result when costs are lower than budgeted: the cost of the materials may have gone down, or the quantity of materials used may have gone down.

An **adverse** (negative) variance will result when costs are higher than budgeted: the cost of the materials may have gone up, or the quantity of materials used may have increased.

## labour variance

**labour variance = standard (budgeted) cost of labour minus actual cost**

Here standard cost is the budgeted total labour cost: the expected number of hours worked multiplied by the appropriate wage rate.

A **favourable** (positive) variance will result when labour costs are lower than budgeted: the wage rate may have gone down (unlikely!), or the number of hours worked may be fewer – the business may have become more efficient.

An **adverse** (negative) variance will result when labour costs are higher than budgeted: there may have been an unexpected wage rise, or the number of hours worked may have increased more than was expected (the machinery or the computer systems may have broken down a lot, leaving people idle).

### overhead variance

The overheads are the running costs of the business.

**overhead variance = standard (budgeted) cost of overheads minus actual cost**

Here standard cost is the budgeted overhead cost: the expected cost of the running expenses of the business.

A **favourable** (positive) variance will result when running costs are lower than budgeted: the business may have switched to a cheaper power company or telephone provider; it may have moved to offices with lower rental.

An **adverse** (negative) variance will result when running costs are higher than budgeted: rates and office rental may have gone up unexpectedly, or the telephone bill may have risen after a telesales campaign.

Note that overheads are either **fixed** and do not vary with the number of items produced (eg office rental) – or **variable** (eg electricity bill) and vary with the volume of items produced. Sometimes a business may calculate separate variances for fixed overheads and variable overheads (see below).

## Activity 6.1

# Investigating variances – costs

|  | standard (budgeted) cost<br>£ | actual cost<br>£ |
| --- | --- | --- |
| materials | 30,000 | 27,000 |
| labour | 60,000 | 75,000 |
| overheads: |  |  |
|   fixed | 30,000 | 27,500 |
|   variable | 10,000 | 11,000 |
| TOTAL COST | 130,000 | 140,500 |

You have been presented with the above cost figures for a manufacturing company.

1   Calculate the variances for the four types of cost.

2   Identify whether they are adverse or favourable.

3   Suggest some factors which might have caused each of the variances.

4   If you were a manager of this business what would you want to investigate?

## Activity 6.2

# Commenting on the sales budget report Premium Soft Drinks

Premium Soft Drinks manufacturers a range of drinks which it distributes throughout the UK.

You are given the following information about Premium's three main brands:

**Sunzest** is a healthy, additive free juice drink based on orange and lemon extracts aimed at the adult market.

**Tingle** is a brightly-coloured fizzy drink, aimed at the children's market.

**Zing** is a carbonated drink, sold in a fashionable can mainly to the teens market.

During the year the following events have occurred:

* all brands have been heavily advertised
* the summer was exceptionally hot
* early in the year there was a health scare over food dyes in children's food and drink
* in the summer a competitor launched a new competitively priced, additive free, children's drink which proved very popular

**You are to:**

1   Write comments on the performance of the three brands shown in the budget report. Explain in each case the factors that have made the variance favourable or adverse, adding any further points which you think might be relevant.

2   State what course of action the manufacturer might take to reverse any adverse trend.

**BUDGET REPORT: Premium Soft Drinks**

**Budget Centre**  Sales Department       **Budget Holder**  R Bolt
**Period**  October 2001                  **Date**  7 November 2001

|  | current period | | | year-to-date | | | trend | comments |
|---|---|---|---|---|---|---|---|---|
|  | budget £000 | actual £000 | variance £000 | budget £000 | actual £000 | variance £000 | | |
| Sunzest | 200 | 250 | + 50 | 2,750 | 3,125 | + 375 | FAV | |
| Tingle | 225 | 200 | - 25 | 1,275 | 1,150 | - 125 | ADV | |
| Zing | 425 | 450 | + 25 | 4,025 | 4,475 | + 450 | FAV | |

## Activity 6.3

# Completing the sales budget report
# Paradise Travel

Paradise Travel is a holiday company which sells UK and foreign holidays largely by telephone, mail order and from its website. During the last few years it has seen considerable growth in foreign holidays, largely because of the poor UK weather and the strength of the pound sterling against other currencies.

The budget for the current year is as follows:

| holiday type | budgeted sales | actual sales | variance | FAV or ADV |
|---|---|---|---|---|
| | £ | £ | £ | |
| UK | 540,000 | | | |
| European Ski | 450,000 | | | |
| European Sun | 670,000 | | | |
| USA Florida Sun | 375,000 | | | |
| USA Ski | 230,000 | | | |
| TOTAL | 2,265,000 | | | |

The sales figures for the present year are shown on the right.

You have been told that a number of factors have affected sales of holidays during the year. These include: a strong pound sterling, bad summer weather in the UK, scare reports about avalanches in the Alps, the popularity

| holiday type | actual sales |
|---|---|
| UK | 496,000 |
| European Ski | 396,000 |
| European Sun | 801,000 |
| USA Florida Sun | 453,000 |
| USA Ski | 286,000 |

of TV 'holiday rep' programmes set in the Mediterranean area, the popularity of Disney theme parks, good snow conditions in the US mountains, cheap US flights.

**You are to:**

1 Draw up a budget report based on the format shown above, enter the actual sales figures and total, work out the variances and state whether they are 'FAV' or 'ADV'.

2 Take each of the types of holiday in turn and link them to the factors listed above.

3 Suggest ways in which any adverse trends, given the same conditions, could be reversed in the coming year.

4 State what could happen to sales in the coming year if the pound sterling fell in value against the US dollar and European currencies before the holiday prices had been fixed.

# the cash budget

If you look at the diagram on page 115 you will see that all the main budgets contribute to the cash budget, which in turn provides the data for the master budget – the forecast financial statements. The cash budget is therefore central to every business: it projects the amounts of money received into and paid out of the bank account each month. A typical cash budget sets out:

• the expected bank account receipts and payments

• on a month-by-month basis

• for a twelve month period

The cash budget (also known as the cash flow forecast) shows projections of all money received and money spent over the year (including VAT), eg sales income, running expenses, payment of tax and purchase of capital items. The 'bottom line' of each monthly column shows the forecast bank balance at the end of that month.

## format of the cash budget

A simplified format of a cash budget, with sample figures, is set out below. Study it carefully and read the explanation which follows.

| Name .............................................Cash Flow Forecast for the ................. months ending ........... | | | | |
|---|---|---|---|---|
| | Jan £000 | Feb £000 | Mar £000 | etc... £000 |
| **Receipts** | | | | |
| sales receipts | 150 | 150 | 161 | 170 |
| other receipts (loans, capital, VAT recovered) | 70 | 80 | 75 | 80 |
| **Total receipts for month (A)** | 220 | 230 | 236 | 250 |
| **Payments** | | | | |
| to suppliers for raw materials or stock (creditors) | 160 | 165 | 170 | 170 |
| other payments (eg expenses, loans repaid, VAT paid) | 50 | 50 | 50 | 60 |
| fixed assets purchased | | 50 | | |
| **Total payments for month (B)** | 210 | 265 | 220 | 230 |
| Opening bank balance at beginning of month | 10 | 20 | (15) | 1 |
| add total receipts (A) | 220 | 230 | 236 | 250 |
| less total payments (B) | 210 | 265 | 220 | 230 |
| **Bank balance (overdraft) at end of month** | 20 | (15) | 1 | 21 |

### receipts

These are analysed for each month to show the amount that is expected to be received from sources such as cash sales, receipts from customers supplied on credit, sale of fixed assets, loans, capital introduced, any interest or other income received. Any refund of VAT received from H M Customs & Excise will also appear in this section.

### payments

This section will show how much is expected to be paid each month for cash purchases, to creditors (suppliers), running expenses, purchases of fixed assets, repayment of capital and loans, and interest paid. If the business is VAT registered, VAT due to H M Customs & Excise will also appear here. (Businesses have to send off the VAT that they charge on invoices).

### bank

The bank summary at the bottom of the budget shows the bank balance at the beginning of the month, to which all receipts are added (A) and payments deducted (B) resulting in the estimated closing bank balance at the end of the month. An overdrawn bank balance is shown in brackets, or by a minus sign.

## timing and the cash budget

The important thing to remember when preparing cash budgets is that receipts and payments are entered in the column for the month in which they are received and paid. This may sound an obvious statement, but if you take into account products sold on credit and products bought on credit you will see that the money often changes hands months after the sale or purchase. Therefore great care must be taken in the following areas:

### credit periods

The cash budget must take into consideration credit periods given on invoices issued and received. For example, if you are told that a business allows two months credit for the products it sells, it means that a sale invoiced in January will be paid for in March and entered as a sales receipt in the cash budget in the March column. In short there is a two month timing lag between sales and sales receipts.

In the same way, if you are told that a business is given one month credit for purchases made (eg stock) it means that a purchase made and invoiced in January will be paid for in February and entered in the cash budget in the February column. Here there is a one month timing lag.

Bills, too, (eg phone and power bills) are entered in the month in which they are paid, even if they apply to periods before or after the payment date.

## constructing the cash budget

We will now explain the various headings which appear in the Receipts and Payments sections of the cash budget by means of a Case Study. This shows how the forecast is constructed and where the figures come from. Note that all figures include VAT where it is charged.

### Case Study

## Merry-go-round Limited
## drawing up the cash budget

Merry-go-round Limited is a small private limited company. It is a family business which makes outdoor toys for children – slides, swings, climbing frames, trampolines and so on. It operates in a leased factory unit on an industrial estate in Broadfield. It supplies stores throughout the UK and also operates a successful factory shop which has the benefit of a cash sales income.

Tom Merry, the Managing Director, is looking to expand the company by purchasing in January new machinery which will enable the business to manufacture its own moulded plastic products. The machinery will cost £50,000 and will be financed partly by a bank loan for £25,000 and partly by new capital of £25,000 introduced by the shareholders (the Merry family). Tom realises that the expansion will also mean that extra working capital is required, and will probably need to be financed by a bank overdraft. The question is, how much cash will the company need?

With the help of his accountant he draws up:

* a capital budget showing the purchase of the new machinery in January of the following year

* a sales budget and a production budget showing the increased sales and costs for the year

He now needs to construct a cash budget to include in the Business Plan which he will take to the bank when he applies for finance. He uses a computer spreadsheet to set out the forecast, with a number of different headings in the receipts and payments sections.

As you read the following descriptions, refer to the cash budget shown on pages 128 and 129

### receipts

**cash sales**
The factory shop is likely to take £8,000 per month in January and February, and then £9,000 a month when the new products are introduced (figures include VAT).

| | |
|---|---|
| **credit sales** | Money received from credit sales is normally received in the month following issue of the invoice. Tom reckons he will receive £18,000 a month in January, February and March, and £25,000 a month for the rest of the year, following the introduction of the new products. |
| **capital** | The shareholders (the Merry family) will introduce £25,000 in January to help finance the new machinery. |
| **loans** | The bank is being asked for a £25,000 business loan to help finance the new machinery in January. |

## payments

| | |
|---|---|
| **raw materials** | These are paid for a month after the invoice date. It is estimated they will cost £15,000 a month for the first four months of the year and £17,000 a month after that. |
| **capital assets** | The new machinery costing £50,000 will be bought and paid for in January. |
| **wages** | The wages bill for the company averages £10,000 a month. |
| **water rates** | Water rates for the year have to be paid for in advance in April. The company's water rates are £1,457. |
| **telephone** | Telephone bills, on the other hand, are paid for quarterly in arrears. On the basis of the previous year's bills they are likely to average £565 a quarter, paid in January, April, July and October. |
| **heat and light** | Gas and electricity bills are also paid for in arrears. They will average in total £650 a quarter, paid in January, April, July and October. |
| **insurance** | The company's comprehensive insurance premium of £7,500 is due in advance in June. |
| **other costs** | Other costs such as office expenses and advertising average £615 a month, paid monthly. |
| **interest costs** | Tom calculates that interest on his borrowing, including any overdraft will be £680 (March), £720 (June), £650 (September), £630 (December). |
| **Loan repayments** | Repayments on bank borrowing are £4,000 a quarter (March, June, September, December). |
| **VAT** | The company is registered for VAT and will have to send a cheque off with the VAT return every quarter. The amount each time will be VAT charged on sales less VAT paid on expenses over the previous three months. |

## totalling up the forecast

When the figures have been entered in the appropriate columns (see the next two pages), the following totals will be calculated by Tom's computer spreadsheet in the far right-hand column and the bank summary at the bottom of the forecast. If a computer spreadsheet is not used, these totals will have to be calculated manually – which is hard work! The figures are:

• totals for each category of receipt or expense in the far right-hand 'total' column (total across each row)

• total receipts for each month, and the far right-hand 'total' column, ie work down the columns

• total payments for each month, and the far right-hand column, ie work down the columns

• cross check the totals for both receipts and payments – ie the total of the monthly columns and the totals in the (far right) total column

• lastly, total monthly receipts and total monthly payments should be entered in the bank position on the appropriate line at the bottom of the forecast

## the bank position

The bank position can now be calculated. Refer to the cash budget on the next two pages as you read this section.

**opening bank balance**   Insert the bank balance at the beginning of January in the row marked 'Opening bank', the figure is £125 in this case.

**add receipts**   Add total receipts for the month.

**deduct payments**   Subtract total payments for the month.

**closing bank**   This is the projected month-end bank balance of the business. It is an overdraft of £4,455 in January. This figure should then also be written in as February's 'Opening Bank' balance. The process is then repeated for February, and so on.

The bottom line of the cash budget shows the all-important figure of the closing bank balance (the expected balance at the end of each month).

A minus figure (or a figure in brackets) indicates an overdraft – ie the business will be borrowing from the bank on its current account.

A positive figure means there is money in the bank account. In this case Merry-go-round Limited will be borrowing on overdraft for most months until August when the borrowing will be repaid.

Now look again at the spreadsheet of the cash budget on the next two pages.

**Cash Budget for Merry-go-round Limited, produced on a spreadsheet**

| | A | B | C | D | E | F | G |
|---|---|---|---|---|---|---|---|
| 1 | CASH BUDGET | | | | | | |
| 2 | Name: Merry-go-round Limited | | | | | | |
| 3 | Period: January - December 2000 | | | | | | |
| 4 | | | | | | | |
| 5 | | Jan | Feb | Mar | Apr | May | Jun |
| 6 | | £ | £ | £ | £ | £ | £ |
| 7 | RECEIPTS | | | | | | |
| 8 | Cash sales | 8000 | 8000 | 9000 | 9000 | 9000 | 9000 |
| 9 | Credit sales | 18000 | 18000 | 18000 | 25000 | 25000 | 25000 |
| 10 | Capital | 25000 | | | | | |
| 11 | Loans | 25000 | | | | | |
| 12 | VAT receipts | | | | | | |
| 13 | Interest | | | | | | |
| 14 | Other income | | | | | | |
| 15 | TOTAL RECEIPTS | 76000 | 26000 | 27000 | 34000 | 34000 | 34000 |
| 16 | | | | | | | |
| 17 | PAYMENTS | | | | | | |
| 18 | Raw materials | 15000 | 15000 | 15000 | 15000 | 17000 | 17000 |
| 19 | Capital assets | 50000 | | | | | |
| 20 | Wages | 10000 | 10000 | 10000 | 10000 | 10000 | 10000 |
| 21 | Water rates | | | | 1457 | | |
| 22 | Telephone | 565 | | | 565 | | |
| 23 | Heat & light | 650 | | | 650 | | |
| 24 | Insurance | | | | | | 7500 |
| 25 | Other costs | 615 | 615 | 615 | 615 | 615 | 615 |
| 26 | Interest costs | | | 680 | | | 720 |
| 27 | Loan repayments | | | 4000 | | | 4000 |
| 28 | VAT payments | 3750 | | | 3885 | | |
| 29 | TOTAL PAYMENTS | 80580 | 25615 | 30295 | 32172 | 27615 | 39835 |
| 30 | | | | | | | |
| 31 | Opening Bank | 125 | -4455 | -4070 | -7365 | -5537 | 848 |
| 32 | Add Receipts | 76000 | 26000 | 27000 | 34000 | 34000 | 34000 |
| 33 | Less Payments | 80580 | 25615 | 30295 | 32172 | 27615 | 39835 |
| 34 | Closing Bank | -4455 | -4070 | -7365 | -5537 | 848 | -4987 |
| 35 | | | | | | | |

| H | I | J | K | L | M | N |
|---|---|---|---|---|---|---|
| Jul | Aug | Sep | Oct | Nov | Dec | TOTAL |
| £ | £ | £ | £ | £ | £ | £ |
| 9000 | 9000 | 9000 | 9000 | 9000 | 9000 | 106000 |
| 25000 | 25000 | 25000 | 25000 | 25000 | 25000 | 279000 |
|  |  |  |  |  |  | 25000 |
|  |  |  |  |  |  | 25000 |
|  |  |  |  |  |  | 0 |
|  |  |  |  |  |  | 0 |
|  |  |  |  |  |  | 0 |
| 34000 | 34000 | 34000 | 34000 | 34000 | 34000 | 435000 |
|  |  |  |  |  |  |  |
| 17000 | 17000 | 17000 | 17000 | 17000 | 17000 | 196000 |
|  |  |  |  |  |  | 50000 |
| 10000 | 10000 | 10000 | 10000 | 10000 | 10000 | 120000 |
|  |  |  |  |  |  | 1457 |
| 565 |  |  | 565 |  |  | 2260 |
| 650 |  |  | 650 |  |  | 2600 |
|  |  |  |  |  |  | 7500 |
| 615 | 615 | 615 | 615 | 615 | 615 | 7380 |
|  |  | 650 |  |  | 630 | 2680 |
|  |  | 4000 |  |  | 4000 | 16000 |
| 4150 |  |  | 4150 |  |  | 15935 |
| 32980 | 27615 | 32265 | 32980 | 27615 | 32245 | 421812 |
|  |  |  |  |  |  |  |
| -4987 | -3967 | 2418 | 4153 | 5173 | 11558 | 125 |
| 34000 | 34000 | 34000 | 34000 | 34000 | 34000 | 435000 |
| 32980 | 27615 | 32265 | 32980 | 27615 | 32245 | 421812 |
| -3967 | 2418 | 4153 | 5173 | 11558 | 13313 | 13313 |

# the cash budget on a computer spreadsheet

## the benefits of a spreadsheet program

The calculations on a cash flow forecast are not particularly difficult, but they do take a long time if you are tackling the task with only pencil, paper and calculator. The task is, of course, made simple when you have input the worksheet onto a computer spreadsheet program. You will be able to change any figure, and the computer will do all the recalculations automatically, for example:

- projections of different levels of sales – optimistic, realistic and pessimistic
- projections of different levels of expenditure
- the effect of buying an asset at different times

In each case you will be able to see the effect on the critical figure of the closing bank balance which indicates the amount of money the business may have to borrow.

## use of formulas in the spreadsheet – column C

Extensive use is made in cash flow forecasts of the adding together of a range of cells. You will need to check your computer manual to find the formula to use for your own program. The formula used here is =Sum(C8:C14) where all the cells between C8 and C14 are added together. The formulas for column C are as follows:

- Rows 15 and 32 – Total Receipts     =Sum(C8:C14)

- Rows 29 and 33 – Total Payments     =Sum(C18:C28)

- Row 31 – Opening Bank     =B34

  – ie the closing bank balance of the previous month. Note that B31 is a value cell into which is entered the opening bank balance for the period.

- Row 34 – Closing Bank     =C31+C32–C33

- Column N – Total column

  Each row is totalled, eg cell N8 is =Sum(B8:M8) and N29 is =Sum(N18:N28). Column N is also totalled vertically, in the same way as the other columns, except that cell N31 is =B31 and cell N34 is =M34. N32 is =Sum(B32:M32) and N33 is =Sum(B33:M33).

## Activity 6.4

# Merry-go-round Limited cash budget on the computer

The tasks in this Activity should be carried out using a computer spreadsheet program. If you are unable to gain access to a suitable system, you should set up the budgets using pencil, paper and calculator, but bear in mind that this will be a more laborious and less flexible alternative.

If you have the time and the opportunity, show the Case Study and completed spreadsheets to a bank lending officer to find out how a lender would react to the proposal.

1  Set up a computer spreadsheet for Merry-go-round Limited and input the figures from the source data in the Case Study. Try to avoid using the finished cash budget! Print out the forecast and check the figures against those shown in the Case Study.

2  The accountant of Merry-go-round Limited is unhappy about presenting a single cash budget to the bank and asks that a "best view" and "worst view" scenario are forecast on the following basis:

(a)  The best view assumes that:
  • cash sales receipts increase to £11,000 per month from March
  • credit sales receipts increase to £28,000 per month from April

(b)  The worst view assumes that the new machine fails to work and that the monthly sales receipts for the year stay at their January level.

You are to set up two new spreadsheet files based on (a) and (b). Amend the sales receipts figures only. For the sake of simplicity do not attempt to adjust any other figures. Print out the two new files.

3  (a)  What do the three forecasts show, and what would be the likely reaction of a lender such as a bank? How would the "best view" and "worst view" alternatives affect the proposed bank loan?

(b)  In the case of the "best view" and "worst view" scenarios, discuss the effect the increase and decrease in sales might have on raw materials purchases, VAT payable and interest payable.

## CHAPTER SUMMARY

- Business planning involves setting objectives for a business.

- The planning process involves four stages:
  - setting the objectives – where the business wants to get to
  - collecting information which will enable the business to assess the present situation
  - making plans which state how the objectives can be achieved
  - monitoring progress, picking up on any problems and taking corrective action

- Objectives can be set out:
  - simply, as in a mission statement for public consumption
  - in a long-term 'corporate plan' which typically runs for five years
  - in a twelve month 'operational plan'

- Operational plans include the setting of budgets by functions within a business (eg sales, production, staffing) and by individual departments.

- Budgets can be income budgets (eg sales budget) or expenditure budgets (eg staffing budget); they are normally expressed in money terms, but can be expressed in units (eg a production budget).

- The budgeting process is determined by 'limiting factors' which are areas which limit the expansion of the business. For example, the amount of the product range which a business can sell will determine the figures that go into the sales budget, which will be the starting point of the planning process.

- The individual budgets combine into the cash budget (which forecasts the flow of money in and out of the business bank account) and the master budget (which sets out a forecast profit and loss account and a forecast balance sheet).

- Budgets must be monitored during the year – often four weekly or monthly. The budget projections will be compared with the actual figures in a budget report and any difference ('variance') will be reported and acted upon. If the actual figures are better than budgeted the variance will be favourable (FAV), if they are worse the variance is adverse (ADV). Managers must look carefully at the causes of any variance and take action accordingly.

- The cash budget shows the flow of money in and out of the bank account and forecasts the bank balance at the end of each month. It is an important budget, not only for management for internal monitoring, but also as a way of presenting the future financial state of the business to a lender such as a bank.

## KEY TERMS

**mission statement**
a public statement made by a business setting out the activities, aims and values of the business

**corporate plan**
a long-term (typically five year) plan which sets out the overall long-term 'strategic' objectives of the business

**operational plan**
a short-term (one year) plan setting targets for specific functional areas within a business; an operational plan will normally contain a budget

**budget**
a table setting out performance targets for a specific area within a business

**functional budget**
a budget for a specific function within a business, eg sales, production, staffing

**departmental budget**
a budget for a specific department within a business

**capital budget**
a budget for the purchase of fixed assets

**cash budget**
a budget projecting the flow of money in and out of the bank account and forecasting the bank balance at the end of each month, also known as the 'cash flow forecast'

**master budget**
the forecast profit and loss account for the year, together with a balance sheet as at the year end

**limiting factor**
an aspect of the business which prevents it from expanding any further

**favourable variance**
the difference between the budgeted figure and the actual figure when the actual figure is better than the forecast figure – often written as 'FAV'

**adverse variance**
the difference between the budgeted figure and the actual figure when the actual figure is not as good as the forecast figure – often written as 'ADV'

# 7

# Control of cash and working capital

Unit 5 Business finance
Cash flow management

## introduction

We saw in the last chapter that the cash budget is a vital management tool in the planning and control of the finance of a business. In this chapter we look more closely at the control of cash and working capital in a business. We examine techniques for improving levels of cash and working capital and avoiding some of the dangers brought about by neglecting the principles of financial control.

## what you will learn from this chapter

- cash passes through a business in a 'money cycle' which involves payments in and out of the bank account, as projected in the cash budget seen in the last chapter

- if the supply of cash coming into the business is restricted the bank account will come under pressure and become overdrawn; if the situation becomes very serious, the business could run out of cash and 'go bust' because it is unable to meet its commitments

- a business also relies on sufficient levels of working capital – this includes cash and also items such as stock and debtors which can be turned into cash; it is calculated as current assets minus current liabilities and measured through performance indicators such as the current and acid test ratios

- a business is able to control and improve its levels of cash and working capital through management of current assets and current liabilities, for example:

  – controlling stock levels to a minimum (stock ties up cash)

  – ensuring debtors pay up on time (releasing the cash needed)

  – paying suppliers as late as possible (hanging onto the cash)

# the cash cycle

## the importance of cash

It is often said that cash is the 'lifeblood' of any business.  When the supply of cash dries up, the business fails.  In this section we look in detail at how cash circulates in the business. As a first step, study the diagram below which shows the cash flowing in and out of a manufacturing business.

Then read the notes on the next page.

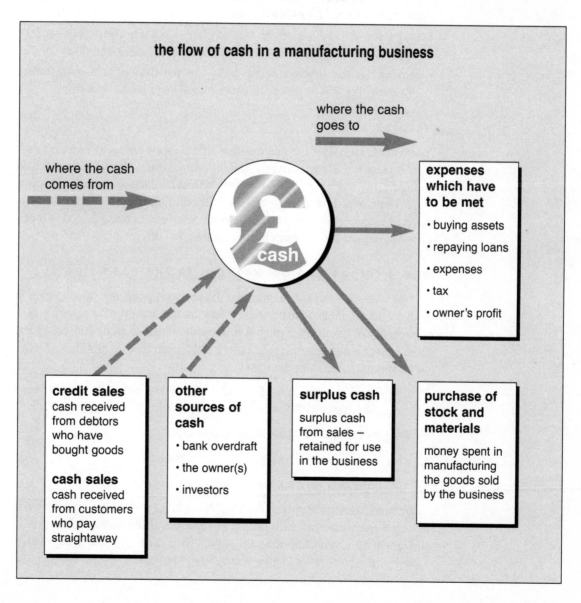

**the flow of cash in a manufacturing business**

where the cash goes to

where the cash comes from

cash

**expenses which have to be met**
- buying assets
- repaying loans
- expenses
- tax
- owner's profit

**credit sales**
cash received from debtors who have bought goods

**cash sales**
cash received from customers who pay straightaway

**other sources of cash**
- bank overdraft
- the owner(s)
- investors

**surplus cash**
surplus cash from sales – retained for use in the business

**purchase of stock and materials**
money spent in manufacturing the goods sold by the business

## where the cash comes from

As you will see from the left-hand side of the diagram on the previous page, there are two main sources of cash:

- cash from the sale of the products of the business – the more the business sells, the more cash it will receive
- cash received from other sources, for example the bank overdraft, cash introduced by the owner(s) or other investors

## where the cash goes

As you will see from the right-hand side of the diagram on the previous page, there are two main 'drains' on the supply of cash:

- expenses which have to be met anyway – buying assets (equipment), repaying loans, paying the owner(s), running expenses and taxation
- paying for the product being sold – in the case of a manufacturing business this will be stocks of raw materials and related expenses

## surplus cash

You will also see from the diagram that a third arrow points to 'surplus cash'. If a business is trading profitably, and the money from sales is being received promptly, the amount of cash over time will exceed the amount being spent. As a result, a cash surplus or residue will build up, possibly in an interest-paying bank account. The business can be described as being 'liquid' – it can afford to pay off the amounts it owes as they fall due.

## where things can go wrong with the cash flow

As you will see from the diagram on the previous page, the flow of cash is vital to the running of a business.  Just as the supply of electricity to a household can be cut off if the bill is not paid, with disastrous consequences, the owner of a business can face failure if the 'cash flow' is not maintained – either from sales or from the bank!

This cycle of money coming in and out of the business can be very precariously balanced.  For example:

- what if sales fall well below the targets set?
- what if a big customer who owes money goes 'bust'?
- what if the bank will not lend any more money on overdraft?

In all these cases the supply of cash will be reduced and the business may not be able to pay important bills or pay its suppliers.  Look at the danger points shown on the diagram on the next page.  Then read the Case Study which follows – it  shows what can go wrong when the supply of cash dries up.

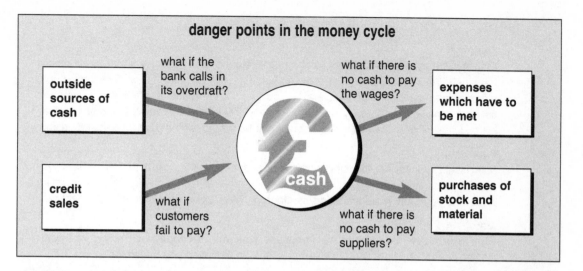

## danger points in the money cycle

| outside sources of cash | → | what if the bank calls in its overdraft? | cash | what if there is no cash to pay the wages? | → | expenses which have to be met |

- **outside sources of cash** — what if the bank calls in its overdraft?
- **credit sales** — what if customers fail to pay?
- what if there is no cash to pay the wages? — **expenses which have to be met**
- what if there is no cash to pay suppliers? — **purchases of stock and material**

## Case Study

# John Spender cash flow problems

### situation

John Spender has started up in business making novelty clocks. He buys quartz clock mechanisms from a wholesaler whom he pays 30 days after he has received the goods and the invoice. He makes the casings from wood and plastic in his workshop. He employs two production workers and does all the marketing, selling and administration himself.

He is very pleased that he has been able to secure contracts to supply a major department store chain and a catalogue mail order company with his clocks. They agree to pay him 60 days after he has supplied and invoiced the goods. He has a £5,000 overdraft with the Albion Bank to provide 'cash flow' for the period after he has paid for his materials, but before he receives payment from his two big customers.

### this is what happens:

**November**

He and his production workers start to work flat out to supply the orders received – which are larger than expected. He has had to order more materials than expected, and his wages bill is bigger.

**December**

He has to pay for his first month's supplies. He has to borrow from the bank on overdraft to pay for them. The bank manager is reasonably happy about this, although he says the amount of £6,000 is larger than he was expecting from John's forecast (his Cash Budget).

**January**

Disaster strikes. The department store's buyer telephones to say that some of the clocks have been returned by their customers complaining that they are faulty. The department store is returning the faulty ones, and will not pay for the remainder until they have been sold. The mail order company, on the other hand, have had no problems, and he receives his first cheque from them. John is so busy that he fails to tell the bank what is happening.

**February**

John issues a cheque to the supplier of the quartz mechanisms, but the bank refuse to pay it, saying that the overdraft is too high – he has borrowed too much already. The supplier refuses to send any more mechanisms. John only has three weeks' supply left in stock.

**March**

John finds that he has to lay off his production workers – he cannot make any more clocks, and he cannot supply orders received. He has no money to pay the workers.

**April**

The bank makes formal demand for its overdraft, which now stands at £8,500; the bank wants its money back. It has a mortgage over John's house, and can sell it if John cannot repay the borrowing.

**May**

John's business fails. He is insolvent – he owes more than he has got.

## Activity 7.1

# Cash flow problems

Read through the John Spender Case Study and answer the following questions:

1   What is the document John has shown to the bank, telling them how much money he is going to need to borrow from them?

2   How much did John think he was going to need to borrow?

3   Why was he going to need this money?

4   Why did the amount of cash needed exceed his initial forecasts (ie before he sent out any goods)?

5   What technical problem occurred which meant that his supply of cash began to run out?

**6** Was it a good idea just to sell to two customers? How could John have solved this problem?

**7** Why did the supplier of quartz mechanisms refuse to supply any more?

**8** Why did John lay off his production workers? What would have happened if he had kept them on?

**9** What was the final 'death blow' to John's business. What could happen to him and his family?

**10** What could John have done to avoid his business failing? Discuss this in class.

## avoiding insolvency

### what is insolvency?

Insolvency is owing more than you have got and being unable to pay debts as they fall due. If the people who are owed money – the creditors – consider they can get their money back through the courts they can do so by:

- making an individual (sole trader or partner) 'bankrupt'
- 'winding up' a company or asking for a company 'administration order'

The end-result of these legal processes is that the assets (belongings) of the individual or company will be sold under court supervision to pay off the creditors.

As you will see from the John Spender Case Study, business failure is often a result of cash flow failure. It is not always entirely the fault of the business owner(s) – bad luck can occur – but good financial management can help.

### how to avoid cash flow failure

Problems caused by cash flow drying up can normally be pinpointed to certain areas. Good management of these areas can help avoid this situation:

- management of debtors – getting them to pay up in good time
- management of creditors – paying suppliers as late as possible (but within the agreed terms!)
- management of stock – not holding onto too much stock

All these items form part of working capital. It is the wider issue of working capital management which we will look at next.

# working capital cycle

## definition of working capital

In the last section we looked at the circulation of cash in a business and the importance of making sure there is enough to meet bills and pay suppliers. Cash is just part of the working capital:

working capital = current assets minus current liabilities

The liquidity of a business – its ability to repay its debts as they fall due – is measured in terms of its ability to raise cash from its current assets, eg by selling stock, by getting its debtors to pay up.

## the working capital cycle

Working capital must keep circulating for a business to survive. The diagram below, which is based on a trading business, shows a series of stages:

1 creditors sell goods to the business on credit

2 stock is sold to customers (debtors) on credit, or for cash (cash sales)

3 debtors make payment and the money is paid into the bank

4 the business pays the creditors from the bank account

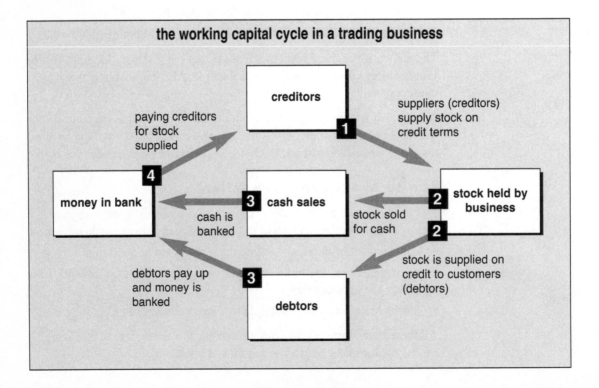

**the working capital cycle in a trading business**

creditors

paying creditors for stock supplied

**4**

suppliers (creditors) supply stock on credit terms

**1**

money in bank

**3** cash sales

cash is banked

stock sold for cash

**2** stock held by business

**2**

stock is supplied on credit to customers (debtors)

debtors pay up and money is banked

**3**

debtors

The bank account will of course also see other payments in (eg loans raised) and payments out (purchase of fixed assets such as computers) which will affect the bank balance. The important point is that the business controls the cycle, as we will see shortly.

## measuring working capital

### accounting ratios

As we saw in Chapter 5, 'Interpreting Financial Information', the current ratio measures the relationship between current assets and current liabilities:

current ratio = current assets : current liabilities

The acid test ratio shows the same relationship but deducts stock from the current assets, taking the view that the stock may be out of date or unsaleable:

acid test ratio = current assets minus stock : current liabilities

Chapter 22 also showed that setting a standard for these ratios has to be viewed with great caution. For example, the normal recommended current ratio of 1.5 : 1 can be thrown out of the window when you look at a shop which sells for cash (and so has no debtors) but buys on credit. Tesco PLC (see page106) actually has a negative working capital!

### working capital cycle

A useful measure of the turn-round of working capital is the working capital cycle measured in days. This is the time lag between the date a business pays for goods it is going to sell and the date it actually gets payment for those goods. Obviously the shorter the time the better from the cash flow point of view. The calculation (with example figures) is:

| working capital cycle | days |
|---|---|
| Time period that goods are in stock on average (nb this is the stock turnover figure - see page 500) | 40 |
| plus | |
| average number of days it takes debtors to pay up (nb this is the debtor collection period - see page 501) | 35 |
| equals | 75 |
| less | |
| average number of days it takes to pay creditors | 30 |
| WORKING CAPITAL CYCLE | 45 |

## Activity 7.2

# Working capital cycle

A farming co-operative grows asparagus in its own farms and supplies a big supermarket chain with fresh asparagus in season. The working capital time periods of the two businesses are:

|  | farmers | supermarket |
|---|---|---|
| Period asparagus in stock (growing and harvesting) | 120 days | 5 days |
| Time period for payment from debtors | 60 days | zero (cash sales) |
| Time taken to pay creditors | 30 days | 60 days |

You are to:

1  Calculate and explain the working capital cycles of the two businesses.

2  Comment on the differences, explaining why there is a difference and suggesting what you would think about the situation if you were a farmer.

## managing working capital

Good working capital management involves:

- **management of debtors** – vetting them in the first place and getting them to pay up in good time

- **management of creditors** – negotiating good prices and discounts, paying suppliers as late as possible, but within the agreed terms

- **management of stock** – not holding onto too much stock, but ensuring that you have enough

These three guidelines clearly apply to manufacturing or retailing businesses which hold stock. The same principles – apart from stock management – apply equally to service industries.

We will now consider each of the principles in turn.

## management of debtors

### checking out the buyer – 'creditworthiness'

When a business sells on credit to a business it has not dealt with before, it needs to make sure that the buyer is likely to be able to pay for the goods or services sold. The buyer must be creditworthy. It is all very well being able to clinch a sale for your product, but if the buyer goes bankrupt after you have delivered the goods, not only will you lose your money, you may well lose the goods as well! There are various ways in which you can 'check out' the buyer's creditworthiness:

- ask for a trade reference from another business which supplies the buyer
- ask for a reference from the buyer's bank

It is normal commercial practice for a buyer to supply these names and addresses to the seller.

If you are selling to a business you can obtain a credit report, for a fee, from a credit reference agency such as Dun & Bradstreet which collects useful business information. Many credit reference agencies nowadays are on-line.

### payment terms

When a business sells goods or services, as we have seen earlier in this chapter, it needs to get the money in as soon as possible. It will have to arrange the most advantageous payment terms. The best terms are a cash sale – the money is received immediately and can be used in the business straightaway.

Normally a business will issue a sales invoice stating the period of time given to the buyer to pay up. The most common period is 30 days. This does not mean, however, that payment will be received then. Businesses often pay on a statement issued at the end of the month. An invoice issued in October will therefore normally be paid after the end of November when the statement is issued. Statistics show that the average payment period in the UK is approximately 45 days.

Some businesses offer a cash discount to buyers: this is a percentage reduction in the bill (often 2.5%) for quick settlement, eg within seven days. Clearly these businesses consider it is better to receive less money straightaway (it costs them 2.5%) rather than wait a month or so and possibly have to borrow that money from a bank and pay bank interest.

You should note that it is an unfortunate fact of business life that large buyers can demand very long payment terms from small sellers who may have to wait up to three months to be paid.

## credit control

An efficient business will keep an eye on its sales ledger (which contains all the debtor accounts), making sure that it receives the money that is owed by sending out reminders, and taking stronger measures if necessary, a process known as credit control. The measures a business might take include:

- statement of account – a document setting out what is owed and when it has to be paid, normally sent out monthly – many businesses pay up on receiving a statement (see page 25 for an example)
- telephone call – some businesses which owe money ignore statements and may need reminding by telephone
- chaser letter – for example "we shall be grateful if you will settle up as soon as possible" or "kindly send your cheque by return of post"
- solicitor's letter – you put the matter in the hands of a solicitor or debt collecting agency who will write to the debtor threatening legal action
- court action – if the amount is large, you can take the matter to the civil courts – but only if you think the debtor has got the money

Good credit control means money in the bank for the business; poor credit control means that the business can lose money – people will tend to pay as late as they can, or in some cases not at all, if they can get away with it! If a debt is not paid it is known as a bad debt and will need to be 'written off'.

## aged debtors analysis

As part of its credit control procedures a business will regularly draw up an aged debtors analysis. This is often done on a monthly basis when the statements are sent out. The aged debtors analysis sets out a list of debtor account balances with a breakdown of how long each debt has been outstanding, eg current (up to 30 days), 30 days (30 to 60 days), 60 days (60 to 90 days) and so on. The person dealing with credit control can therefore easily identify amounts that need to be chased up in various ways. The longer the period the stronger the remedy. Look at the example shown below.

| HELICON LIMITED | AGED DEBTORS ANALYSIS | | | | | | 30 June 2000 |
| --- | --- | --- | --- | --- | --- | --- | --- |
| Account | Turnover | Credit Limit | Balance | Current | 30 days | 60 days | Older |
| Hedley Turner & Co | 370.00 | 1000.00 | 164.50 | 164.50 | 0.00 | 0.00 | 0.00 |
| Hinchcliff & Co | 320.00 | 750.00 | 376.00 | 376.00 | 0.00 | 0.00 | 0.00 |
| Maxwell Nurseries | 1730.00 | 1000.00 | 1632.75 | 799.00 | 833.75 | 0.00 | 0.00 |
| Henry James Trading | 2025.00 | 1500.00 | 1926.88 | 880.00 | 46.88 | 1000.00 | 0.00 |
| R Patel | 425.00 | 750.00 | 499.38 | 499.38 | 0.00 | 0.00 | 0.00 |
| TOTALS | 4870.00 | 5000.00 | 4599.51 | 2718.88 | 880.63 | 1000.00 | 0.00 |

## Activity 7.3

# Chasing the debtors

Study the aged debtor analysis shown on the previous page and answer the questions set out below. The standard payment terms for customers is 30 days.

1   Which two accounts might give the credit controller cause for concern, and why?

2   If you were the credit controller what would you do to deal with these accounts?

## managing the suppliers

### long credit

Businesses should always try to obtain as long a credit period as possible (ie pay as late as possible). This will help the flow of working capital. If it is possible, for example, to pay a supplier after sixty days rather than thirty, the amount owed will be available for use in the buyer's business as cash. Alternatively, if the buyer is borrowing from the bank on overdraft, a delay in settling a bill will mean borrowing less, and paying less interest. A business should, however, beware of taking liberties and making a habit of paying later than the due date – the seller may cut off credit altogether!

### negotiating terms

It is possible to haggle over prices. It may also be possible to get one supplier to match the price of another (just as many electrical retailers will 'match' the price of another). The less a business has to pay for its supplies, the more working capital will be available.

### managing stock

Holding stock costs money and is a drain on working capital, so businesses must steer a middle course between holding too much stock and holding too little stock.

If a business has a high level of stock, cash will have been paid out to finance it – cash which could have been put to better use in the business.

Also, a high level of stock may need a larger warehouse or premises than is necessary, and stockholding costs will be higher.

If on the other hand too little stock is held, sales will be lost if an item is out of stock because the customer will go elsewhere. Some businesses, particularly those in the manufacturing sector, operate a *just-in-time (JIT)* method which, as the name suggests, replaces stock just before it will be needed. This works well until the supply unexpectedly comes to a halt, for example when a natural disaster halts the supply of microchips for computers.

A business therefore needs efficient stock control which will strike the balance between holding too much stock and too little stock. This can be achieved by setting maximum and minimum stockholding quantities for each item of stock and deciding on appropriate re-order quantities.

## Activity 7.4

# Rally Bats Limited
# working capital management

Ben Dawes is the managing director of Rally Bats Limited, a company which makes table tennis bats which he sells to wholesalers and also by mail order.

The company's balance sheet has just been prepared by the accountant. Ben says to you that he never seems to have much cash to take out for his salary.

He says that he has been asked to meet the bank manager next week because the bank account seems to be permanently overdrawn.

Ben shows you the working capital figures, his latest year-end aged debtors summary and the performance figures for debtors collection, stock turnover and creditor payment.

|  | last year | this year |
|---|---|---|
|  | £ | £ |
| Stock | 6,500 | 8,910 |
| Debtors | 15,250 | 25,800 |
| Bank account | 1,270 | (7,810) |
| Creditors | 5,685 | 14,780 |

| RALLY BATS LIMITED | | AGED DEBTORS ANALYSIS | | | | |
|---|---|---|---|---|---|---|
| Account | Credit Limit | Balance | Current | 30-60 days | 61-90 days | older |
| LLB Sports | 1000.00 | 2100.00 | 100.00 | 500.00 | 1000.00 | 500.00 |
| Baylis Trading | 5000.00 | 5050.00 | 2500.00 | 0.00 | 0.00 | 2550.00 |
| R&S Wholesale | 10000.00 | 12560.00 | 00.00 | 10590.00 | 1970.00 | 0.00 |
| P J Smith Ltd | 5500.00 | 4,575.00 | 880.00 | 2695.00 | 1000.00 | 0.00 |
| Antonio Supplies | 2000.00 | 1515.00 | 500.00 | 650.00 | 365.00 | 0.00 |
| TOTALS | 23500.00 | 25,800.00 | 3980.00 | 14435.00 | 4335.00 | 3050.00 |

| | last year | this year |
|---|---|---|
| Stock turnover (days) | 50 | 79 |
| Debtor collection (days) | 40 | 65 |
| Creditors payments (days) | 42 | 60 |

**You are to**

1   Calculate his working capital for the two years.

2   Calculate his current ratio for the two years.

3   Calculate his acid test ratio for the two years.

4   Calculate his working capital cycle (in days) for the two years.

5   Comment on the performance indicators you have calculated in 1-4 above.

6   Suggest ways in which he could improve his working capital management.

## CHAPTER SUMMARY

- The availability of cash in a business is essential to its continuing operation. It passes through a business in a 'cash cycle' which involves payments in and out of the bank account, as projected in the cash budget.

- Sources of cash include income from the sale of its products or from other sources such as loans and the owner investing capital.

- The cash flows out to pay for essential purchases such as stock, running expenses and other assets which the business buys from time to time.

- Problems can arise with the flow of cash if sales decline, if customers fail to pay and loans are refused. In the worst case the business can go 'bust'.

- Cash is one of the elements of working capital which also includes debtors and stock among its assets as sources of cash.

- The working capital cycle expands on the idea of the cash cycle. In the case of a trading business it involves four stages:
  - creditors sell goods to the business on credit
  - the goods are sold to customers on credit, or for cash
  - debtors make payment and the money is paid into the bank
  - the business pays the creditors from the bank account

- The working capital cycle can be measured (in days) by adding the average time stock is held to the average time it takes debtors to pay up, and then deducting the average time it takes to pay creditors. This is the time lag between the date a business pays for goods it is going to sell and the date on which it gets payment.

- Careful management of the main elements of working capital – debtors, creditors and stock – is essential to the efficient working of the business.

- Debtors are a source of cash, so it is critical that they are not allowed to get away with delaying payment. Debtor management – known as credit control – involves 'vetting' customers in the first place and then monitoring payments through the sales ledger by means of an aged debtors summary.

- Creditors are a drain on cash, so it is useful if a business can pay as late as it can (without jeopardising the trading relationship). Creditor management therefore involves making sure that the business gets the best deal from its suppliers in terms of pricing and being able to pay as late as possible.

- Stock costs money to hold, so stock management – known as stock control – has as its main aim to hold just enough stock, and not too much or too little.

## KEY TERMS

**cash cycle** — the flow of cash in and out of a business bank account

**cash budget** — a budget projecting the flow of money in and out of the bank account and forecasting the bank balance at the end of each month

**insolvency** — being unable to pay debts as and when they fall due

**working capital** — current assets minus current liabilities – the funds available to finance the day-to-day working of a business

**working capital cycle** — the time lag between the date a business pays for goods it is going to sell and receiving payment for those goods

**creditworthiness** — the ability of a debtor to pay for products supplied

**credit control** — the management of the sales ledger (debtor accounts) to ensure prompt payment of sales invoices issued

**aged debtor summary** — a list of debtor account balances with a breakdown of how long each debt has been outstanding

**long credit** — the negotiation of payment terms as late as possible

**stock control** — management of the levels of stock within a business, ensuring that:
- stock is ordered when necessary
- high stock levels are avoided

**Just-In-Time (JIT)** — the policy of replacing stock just before it will be needed, and not before

# 8 Financial analysis and planning

## introduction

One of the most important parts of the business plan is the financial section. This sets out the sources of finance and shows how the planned product will be financially viable. It does this by means of financial forecasts and a calculation analysing when sales of the product will break-even and costs will be covered.

## what you will learn from this chapter

● there are a number of different sources of finance for a business: some are internal (such as personal savings) and others are external (such as bank loans)

● when a business raises finance it will normally match the repayment period of the finance to the life of the asset, for example using an overdraft for working capital and a ten year loan for machinery

● the financial section of a business plan should contain six sections:

1　the sources of finance – where the money is coming from

2　estimates of the money  needed, both for start-up costs and also for running costs

3　a break-even calculation

4　a cash flow forecast over a twelve month period

5　a forecast operating budget (profit statement) over a twelve month period

6　a start-up balance sheet

● a business will need to extract performance ratios on a regular basis in order to evaluate its success

## sources of finance

Finance is normally needed for starting a business, buying a business, or expanding a business. Finance can be internal (from the owner's savings and capital or from profits), or external (from a bank, for example).

### matching the finance to the assets

Lenders will normally want to match the period of any lending to the expected life of the asset financed. There are three generally accepted timescales for finance, although you may find definitions which will vary from these:

| | | |
|---|---|---|
| short-term | 1 to 2 years | short-term requirements, ie working capital |
| medium-term | 3 to 10 years | purchase of fixed assets, eg machinery |
| long-term | 11 to 25 years | purchase of land and premises |

As you will see, the longer the life of the asset purchased, the longer the loan that will be made available.

## borrowing from the bank

### types and sources of finance

We will now consider the various types and sources of finance. It should be noted that some of the sources listed here only provide finance to limited companies: this will be made clear in the text.

The banks are the largest providers of finance to all types of businesses. Forms of lending vary from bank to bank, and you should investigate the various schemes available and when they have to be repaid. A bank will be able to arrange, by itself, or through specialised companies which it owns:

- overdrafts
- factoring services
- short and medium-term loans ('business loans')
- leasing for equipment purchase and hire purchase
- commercial mortgages
- venture capital

### interest on borrowing

Interest is paid on money borrowed and is calculated as a percentage of the amount borrowed. Banks normally set their interest rates at a set percentage (which varies according to the risk element in the lending) above the prevailing Base Rate. Base Rate is varied periodically at the direction of the Bank of England in order to 'fine-tune' the amount of borrowing in the economy. The reason for this is that interest is a cost to the business, and when interest rates are high they can restrict the amount a business can afford to borrow.

### bank working capital finance

#### overdraft

An overdraft is short-term borrowing on a bank current account. It is relatively cheap because you only pay interest on what you actually borrow. You normally pay an arrangement fee when an overdraft is set up.

A 'limit' up to which you can borrow will be granted by the bank, and reviewed annually, when it can be increased, decreased or renewed at the same level. A renewal fee is payable for this service.

An overdraft is the most common form of finance for working capital. It provides the finance when a business needs to pay creditors or meet other short-term bills.

### finance arranged through bank-owned companies

Finance houses, which are specialist companies owned in the main by the major banks, offer alternative ways of obtaining fixed assets:

#### hire purchase

An HP agreement from a finance house enables a business to acquire an asset on the payment of a deposit and to pay back the cost plus interest over a set period, at the end of which ownership of the asset passes to the borrower. Hire purchase is often used to finance vehicles and machinery.

#### leasing

Leasing arrangements are also provided by finance houses. With a leasing agreement, the business has use of assets such as cars and computers bought by the finance house. The business pays a regular 'rental' payment, normally over a lease period of two to seven years. Ownership of the asset does not normally pass to the business because the asset (the car, the computer) will have become out-of-date and will need renewing at the end of the lease period. Clearly a lease is not a loan, but it can substantially reduce the financial requirements of a business when it needs to acquire assets such as computer equipment and fleets of company cars.

## factoring – working capital finance

Many banks also provide factoring services through specialist factoring companies. A business may have valuable financial resources tied up because its customers owe it money and have not yet paid. A factoring company will effectively 'buy' these debts by providing a number of services:

• it will lend up to 80% of outstanding customer debts

• it will deal with all the paperwork of collecting customer debts

• it can in some instances insure against non-payment of debts

Factoring frees money due to the business and allows the business to use it in its general operations and expansion plans. It is therefore a valuable source of short-term finance.

## bank fixed asset finance

### business loan

This is a fixed medium-term loan, typically for between 3 and 10 years, to cover the purchase of capital items such as machinery or equipment. Interest is normally 2% to 3% over base rate, and repayments are by installments.

### commercial mortgage

If you are buying premises for your business you can arrange to borrow long-term by means of a commercial mortgage, typically up to 80% of the value of the property, repayable over a period of up to 25 years. Your premises will be taken as security for the loan: if the business fails, the premises will be sold to repay the bank.

### finance for companies: venture capital

There are many specialist banks – 'merchant banks' – and investment companies which offer advice and financial assistance to limited companies looking for capital. This financial assistance takes the form of loans and venture capital which provides finance for fixed assets and for working capital. Venture capital companies will view these companies as investment opportunities and will put in money in the form of loans or purchase of shares, or both. In return, they may expect an element of control over the company and will possibly insist on having a director on the board of the company. A venture capital company considering investing will look for a business with a good sales and profit record – or potential.

# financial assistance from the Government

The UK Government provides financial help – Regional Selective Assistance – to businesses setting up in areas which have traditionally had higher levels of unemployment and low earnings. This assistance – grants, cheap rents, free and subsidised advice – is administered through the Department of Trade and Industry, which is often referred to as the DTI. The areas given assistance are known as the Assisted Areas. □They are shown as shaded areas on the map shown below. They are divided into three 'tiers':

### Tier 1 (dark shading)

These are the areas of greatest need and include Cornwall, Merseyside, South Yorkshire, West Wales, the Welsh Valleys and all of Northern Ireland (not shown on the map).

### Tier 2 (light shading)

These are local areas of need. They do not qualify for grants as high as those in Tier 1.

### Tier 3 (not shown on the map)

This applies to businesses employing up to 250 people in certain areas of the UK.

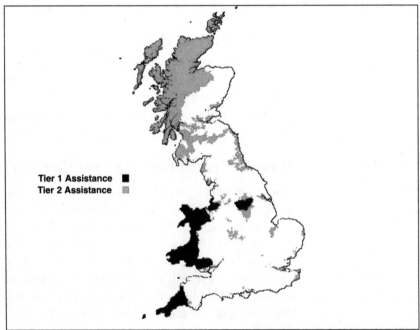

Source: Department of Trade and Industry

The Assisted Areas (provisional map published in 2000)

## a financial needs schedule

A business plan will often summarise in a schedule (see below):

- the need for fixed assets and working capital (such as stock and money in the bank)
- the sources of finance used to pay for them – these could include bank finance, grants and money invested by the owner(s)

### financial needs

| Item needed | £ |
|---|---|
| office premises | 125,000 |
| computers | 45,000 |
| office equipment | 12,500 |
| vehicle | 12,500 |
| working capital | 40,000 |
| TOTAL COST OF PROJECT | 235,000 |

| to be provided by | £ |
|---|---|
| own resources | 125,000 |
| bank finance: | |
| commercial mortgage for office | 50,000 |
| business loan for computers | 20,000 |
| overdraft for working capital | 40,000 |
| TOTAL OF FINANCING | 235,000 |

## Activity 8.1

# Investigating types of finance

What alternative forms of financing could you suggest for the business shown in the above schedule for the following needs? Assume that the business is a limited company.

1   Working capital – bearing in mind that the business sells on credit.

2   Computers –  the business may need to replace them every two or three years.

3   Share capital – the owner says he may be looking for outside investors.

# budgeting for income and costs

## the need for budgets

In Chapter 23 we looked at the need for businesses to budget – to estimate – for income and spending in different areas of a business. If the business is starting up for the first time or expanding its product line it will need to budget for sales income and for costs in areas such as marketing, production (or operations if it is a service business), and human resources (staffing).

It is clear that pricing must take into account the costs which the business will incur. These will include variable costs and fixed costs (overheads).

## budgeting for variable costs and gross profit

Certain costs will be directly related to the number of items – a manufactured item or a service – produced by the business. These are known as **variable costs** or **cost of sales**. They might include costs such as:

- raw materials and components (for a manufacturer)
- stocks of items to sell in a shop (for a retailer)
- sales commission paid to sales reps

The business will need to make sure that it makes a profit when fixing its price. The first measure of profit is gross profit:

$$\text{GROSS PROFIT} = \text{SALES} - \text{VARIABLE COSTS}$$

As we saw in Chapter 5, gross profit is measured in percentage terms as gross profit margin:

$$\text{GROSS PROFIT MARGIN} = \frac{\text{GROSS PROFIT} \times 100\%}{\text{SALES}}$$

If, therefore, a business has budgeted sales income of £200,000 and variable costs (cost of sales) of £120,000, it will have a gross profit of £200,000 minus £120,000 = £80,000 gross profit. Its gross profit margin will be:

$$\frac{\text{£80,000 (gross profit)} \times 100\%}{\text{£200,000 (sales)}} = 40\%$$

This means that for every £10 of sales, £4 is profit once variable costs (cost of sales) have been paid off.

The business then has to pay off its fixed costs, known as overheads.

## budgeting for fixed costs and net profit

There will be certain costs a business will have to pay, even if it produces no product or service at all. These are fixed costs, also known as overheads. If you are budgeting for a new business or product you should allow for fixed costs such as:

- premises – rent or loan repayments, insurance, security, rates
- services such as electricity, gas, telephone
- wages and salaries of permanent staff
- marketing and advertising, travel, postage, stationery
- depreciation – wear and tear on equipment

The business will want to make sure that the gross profit it has made (sales less the variable costs) will cover the fixed costs, or it will make a loss. Let us assume that the yearly total of all the fixed costs listed above is £60,000.

The second measure of profit is net profit:

$$\text{NET PROFIT} = \text{GROSS PROFIT} - \text{FIXED COSTS (OVERHEADS)}$$

As we saw in Chapter 22, net profit is measured in percentage terms as net profit margin:

$$\text{NET PROFIT MARGIN} = \frac{\text{NET PROFIT} \times 100\%}{\text{SALES}}$$

If we look again at the business illustrated on the previous page, it will have a net profit of £80,000 (the gross profit) minus £60,000 (the fixed costs) = £20,000 net profit. Its net profit margin will be:

$$\frac{£20,000 \text{ (net profit)} \times 100\%}{£200,000 \text{ (sales)}} = 10\%$$

This means that for every £10 of sales, £1 is profit once all the costs (both variable and fixed costs) have been paid off.

## Activity 8.2

# Measuring profitability

You have drawn up budgets for two different business ideas. The first will manufacture garden tools, the second will run two hairdressing salons. Which is more profitable? Work out the gross and net profit margins. Which business idea seems better, and why?

1  Annual sales £400,000, variable costs £280,000, fixed costs £80,000.

2  Annual sales £200,000, variable costs £80,000, fixed costs £80,000.

# financial forecasts in the business plan

Budgeting involves drawing up estimates of:

- sales income for the year
- variable costs for the year
- fixed costs for the year

Once these figures have been established – and remember that they are only estimates – the business plan can move forwards with the production of three important forecasts:

### the break-even calculation

This will enable the business to know exactly how much sales income it needs to cover its costs. Obviously if the business cannot cover its costs it needs to re-think the proposition.

### the operating budget (forecast profit and loss account)

This projects the level of profits expected on a year's trading. It lists the sales income and both variable and fixed costs.

### the cash flow forecast (cash budget)

This has already been explained in detail in Chapter 6. It projects the flows of money in and out of the bank account of the business during the year. It will pick up any times when the business will be short of cash – a dangerous occurrence in any business, but particularly so in a start-up situation.

We will look at these three projections in turn.

# will the business break-even?

### the concept of break-even

A business planning a new project is only likely to go ahead if it is eventually going to make a profit on that project. It will make a profit after it has broken even – as soon as its sales income covers its running costs. Note that break-even is only concerned with running costs – not start-up costs.

Break-even is therefore the point at which running costs are covered by the income received. After that point you are making a profit. A definition is:

*break-even is the point at which sales income is equal to running costs*

# two ways of calculating break-even

There are two ways of calculating break-even:

## by formula

These are basic calculations which use budgeted figures such as the gross profit margin percentage, variable costs and fixed costs.

## by graph

This is a more sophisticated method which takes more time, but which provides the business with a great deal more information.

## break-even by formula

### 1. to find out the level of sales in £ needed to break-even

The information you will need for the first calculation is the fixed costs (overheads) and the gross profit margin percentage. If you do not have the gross profit margin percentage, it can be calculated by dividing the gross profit by the sales and multiplying by 100. The break-even formula is:

$$\frac{\text{FIXED COSTS}}{\text{GROSS PROFIT MARGIN}} \times 100 = \text{BREAK-EVEN LEVEL OF SALES}$$

So taking the business we looked at on page 596, if gross profit margin is 40% and fixed costs are £60,000, the calculation is:

$$\frac{£60,000}{40} \times 100 = £150,000 \text{ OF SALES NEEDED TO BREAK-EVEN}$$

Projected sales for the period are £200,000, so the business has to achieve 75% of its target before it covers its running costs.

### 2. to find out the number of units to sell to break-even

When the business has worked out the number of units (items or services) it plans to sell over the first year of trading, it can use the following formula to work out the number of items it will need to sell to break-even:

$$\frac{\text{FIXED COSTS}}{\text{SELLING PRICE PER UNIT minus VARIABLE COST PER UNIT}}$$

=     NUMBER OF UNITS NEEDED TO BREAK-EVEN

### the break-even graph

A business is likely to find the calculation by formula on the previous page useful, but will point out its limitations. The management might ask questions like:

*"How much profit will we make if we sell 200 more units per month than the break-even amount?"*

*"How much loss will we make if production is short of the break-even point by 100 units."*

The answer is to be found in the construction of a break-even graph which plots units of production on the horizontal axis and sales and costs on the vertical axis. This graph shows:

- a total cost line which is the sum of fixed and variable costs
- a sales revenue line which rises from zero

## Case Study

# Prontoys Limited
## drawing a break-even graph

Prontoys Limited is launching a new cuddly toy know as 'Wuffles'. It has decided to draw a break-even graph to check the feasibility of the scheme. Before a break-even graph can be constructed, a table will be drawn up setting out the income and costs for different numbers of units. A table for Wuffles is shown below. The data used is: selling price per unit £20, variable cost per unit £10, fixed costs per month £5,000. Some of the figures from the table are then used to plot straight lines on the graph. These are:

- the total cost line (Column C)
- the sales income line (Column D)

| units of production | fixed costs | variable costs | total cost | sales income | profit/(loss) |
|---|---|---|---|---|---|
| | A | B | C | D | E |
| | | | A + B | | D – C |
| | £ | £ | £ | £ | £ |
| 100 | 5,000 | 1,000 | 6,000 | 2,000 | (4,000) |
| 200 | 5,000 | 2,000 | 7,000 | 4,000 | (3,000) |
| 300 | 5,000 | 3,000 | 8,000 | 6,000 | (2 000) |
| 400 | 5,000 | 4,000 | 9,000 | 8,000 | (1,000) |
| 500 | 5,000 | 5,000 | 10,000 | 10,000 | nil |
| 600 | 5,000 | 6,000 | 11,000 | 12,000 | 1,000 |
| 700 | 5,000 | 7,000 | 12,000 | 14,000 | 2,000 |

## notes on the break-even table

- the units of production here are at intervals of 100
- fixed costs (Column A) are fixed at £5,000 for every level of production
- fixed costs (Column A) and variable costs (Column B) are added together to produce the total cost figure (Column C)
- total cost (Column C) is deducted from the sales income figure (Column D) to produce either a positive figure (a profit) or a loss (a negative figure, in brackets) in Column E

As you can see, break-even occurs at 500 units.

## construction of the break-even graph

The graph is constructed as follows:

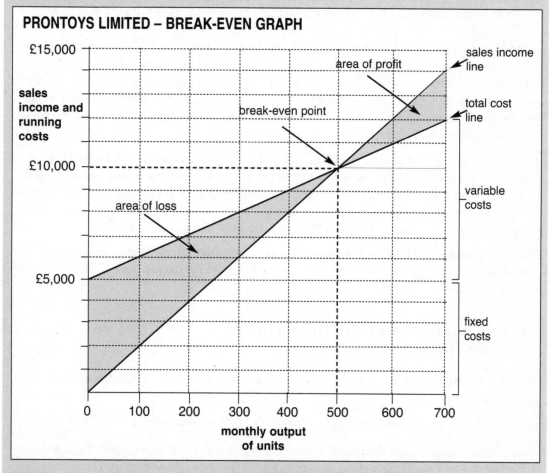

Study the format of the graph and then read the notes on the next page.

## notes on the break even graph

- The vertical axis shows money amounts – the total cost and the sales income for different levels of production are plotted on this axis.

- The horizontal axis shows units of output at intervals of 100.

- The fixed costs of £5,000 are the same at all levels of output.

- Total cost is made up of fixed costs and variable costs.

- The total costs line starts, not at zero, but at £5,000. This is because if the output is zero, the business still has to pay the £5,000 fixed costs.

- The point at which the total costs and sales income lines cross is the break-even point.

- From the graph you can read off the break-even point both in terms of units of output (500 units on the horizontal axis) and also in sales income value (£10,000 on the vertical axis).

## working out profit and loss from the graph

If you look at the graph on the previous page you will see two shaded areas. On the left of the break-even point is an 'area of loss' and on the right of the break-even point is an 'area of profit'. This means that for levels of output to the left of the break-even point (ie fewer than 500 units) the business will make a loss and for levels of output to the right of the break-even point, the business will make a profit.

If you read off the vertical distance (in £) between the sales income line and the total cost line (ie down the shaded area) you will find the exact amount of profit and loss for any level of output on the graph. Note that each dotted 'box' on the graph represents £1,000 from top to bottom. For example, at an output level of zero you will make a loss of £5,000 (this is the fixed costs figure) and at an output level of 700 units you will make a profit of £2,000.

If you refer back to the table of figures from which the graph was plotted (page 160) you will be able to check these figures taken from the graph against the expected profit and loss totals in the far right-hand column.

## how the graph helps Prontoys Limited

The questions asked by the management were:

"How much profit will we make if we sell 200 more Wuffles per month than the break-even amount?"

"How much loss will we make if production is short of the break-even point by 100 units."

By reading the difference between the total cost line and the total income line, the answer to the first question is £2,000 and the answer to the second is a loss of £1,000.

## Activity 8.3

# Reading a break-even graph

You have been given a break-even graph for Insight Limited. Study the graph and answer the questions at the bottom of the page.

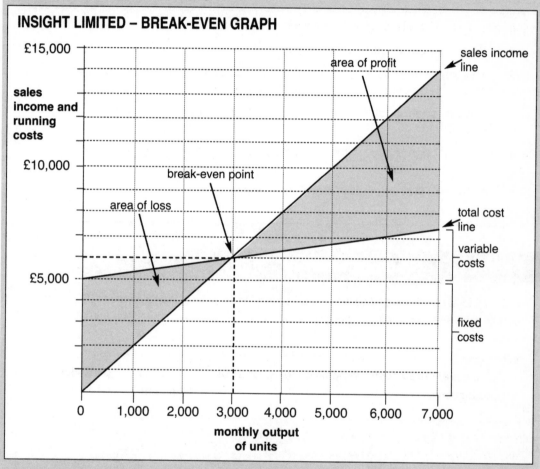

**INSIGHT LIMITED – BREAK-EVEN GRAPH**

1   How many units does Insight Limited have to produce to break even?

2   What are the fixed costs at the break-even point?

3   What are the variable costs at the break-even point?

4   What loss does Insight Limited make when output is zero units?

5   Why is this loss made?

6   What profit is made by Insight Limited when the output is 6,000 units?

## Activity 8.4

# Drawing a break-even graph

You have been given the projected monthly figures for two businesses and have been asked to construct break-even graphs for both of them. You have also been given a sheet of paper with hints for drawing break-even graphs.

### hints for drawing break-even graphs

1   Use graph paper and a sharp pencil.

2.  You only need to plot two points for each line, one at zero output and one at maximum output. The lines will always be straight.

3.  Allow enough space on the vertical axis for the highest of the sales income figures.

4.  Allow enough space on the horizontal axis for the highest of the units of production figures.

5.  Make sure that your graph is correctly labelled.

## business 1: Framers Limited

Framers Limited makes and sells framed Pop Art Posters. The selling price is £20 per framed poster, the variable cost is £10 per poster and the monthly fixed costs total £3,000.

| units of production | fixed costs | variable costs | total cost | sales income | profit/(loss) |
|---|---|---|---|---|---|
| | A | B | C | D | E |
| | | | A + B | | D – C |
| | £ | £ | £ | £ | £ |
| 0 | 3,000 | 0 | 3,000 | 0 | (3,000) |
| 100 | 3,000 | 1,000 | 4,000 | 2,000 | (2,000) |
| 200 | 3,000 | 2,000 | 5,000 | 4,000 | (1,000) |
| 300 | 3,000 | 3,000 | 6,000 | 6,000 | nil |
| 400 | 3000 | 4,000 | 7,000 | 8,000 | 1,000 |
| 500 | 3,000 | 5,000 | 8,000 | 10,000 | 2,000 |
| 600 | 3,000 | 6,000 | 9,000 | 12,000 | 3,000 |
| 700 | 3,000 | 7,000 | 10,000 | 14,000 | 4,000 |
| 800 | 3,000 | 8,000 | 11,000 | 16,000 | 5,000 |

## tasks

1    Calculate the break-even point using the formula method to check the accuracy of the table on the previous page. The formula for the break-even quantity of output is:

$$\frac{\text{fixed costs (£)}}{\text{selling price per unit (£) less variable cost per unit (£)}}$$

2    Draw up a break-even graph, using the hints set out on the previous page.

3    Read off the graph the profit or loss if 100 posters are produced and sold each month.

4    Read off the graph the profit or loss if 600 posters are produced and sold each month.

5    Check the answers to 3 & 4 against the figures in the table on the previous page.

## business 2: Winthrop Furniture

Winthrop Furniture makes and sells a wooden garden seat known as the 'Eden'. The figures for this business have not yet been set out in the form of a table. All you have been given are the following monthly figures:

| | |
|---|---|
| Cost of timber and labour for making seat | £20 per seat |
| Selling price | £45 per seat |
| Monthly fixed costs | £15,000 |

## tasks

1    Draw up a table showing fixed costs, variable costs, total costs, sales income, and profit or loss for production of seats in multiples of 100 from zero up to 1,000.

2    Calculate the break-even point using the formula method to check your workings. The formula for the break-even quantity of output is:

$$\frac{\text{fixed costs (£)}}{\text{selling price per unit (£) less variable cost per unit (£)}}$$

3    Draw up a break-even graph, using the hints set out on the previous page.

4    Read off the graph the profit or loss if 200 seats are produced and sold each month.

5    Read off the graph the profit or loss if 1,000 seats are produced and sold each month.

6    Check the answers to 4 & 5 against the figures in the table produced in question 1.

# the cash flow forecast

> This financial forecast is explained in full in Chapter 6, pages 123 to 129. You should read these pages again to remind yourself how a cash flow forecast works. Also study the format of the forecast shown below and read the revision notes that follow.

The cash flow forecast (also known as cash budget) shows projections of all money received and money spent over the year, for example sales income, running expenses, start-up costs. In short, everything that passes through the bank account is shown in the cash flow forecast. The 'bottom line' of each monthly column shows the forecast bank balance at the end of that month.

## its place in the business plan

The cash budget is possibly the most important financial statement in the Business Plan which is presented to a prospective lender in an application for finance. It shows what amount needs to be borrowed and when. If the figures show that the bank balance will move into credit, it provides the lender with confidence that borrowing can be repaid, and also gives the owner confidence that targets can be met.

| Name .............................................Cash Flow Forecast for the ................. months ending ........... | | | | |
|---|---|---|---|---|
| | Jan £000 | Feb £000 | Mar £000 | etc... £000 |
| **Receipts** | | | | |
| sales receipts | 150 | 150 | 161 | 170 |
| other receipts (loans, capital, VAT recovered) | 70 | 80 | 75 | 80 |
| **Total receipts for month (A)** | 220 | 230 | 236 | 250 |
| **Payments** | | | | |
| to suppliers for raw materials or stock (creditors) | 160 | 165 | 170 | 170 |
| other payments (eg expenses, loans repaid, VAT paid) | 50 | 50 | 50 | 60 |
| fixed assets purchased | | 50 | | |
| **Total payments for month (B)** | 210 | 265 | 220 | 230 |
| Opening bank balance at beginning of month | 10 | 20 | (15) | 1 |
| add total receipts (A) | 220 | 230 | 236 | 250 |
| less total payments (B) | 210 | 265 | 220 | 230 |
| **Bank balance (overdraft) at end of month** | 20 | (15) | 1 | 21 |

### receipts

These are analysed for each month to show the amount that is expected to be received from sources such as cash sales, receipts from customers supplied on credit, sale of fixed assets, loans, capital introduced, VAT recovered, and any interest or other income received.

### payments

This section will show how much is expected to be paid each month for cash purchases, to creditors (suppliers), running expenses, purchases of fixed assets, repayment of capital and loans, interest paid and tax paid.

### bank

The Bank summary at the bottom of the budget shows the bank balance at the beginning of the month, to which all receipts are added (A) and payments deducted (B) resulting in the estimated closing bank balance at the end of the month. An overdrawn bank balance is shown in brackets, or by a minus sign.

Remember that the figures included and calculated are always estimates. It is important to be realistic for these estimates.

# the forecast profit and loss account

Another important forecast which is included in the Business Plan is the forecast profit and loss account. Whereas the cash flow forecast shows all receipts and all payments (including start-up costs, loans received, and owner's capital introduced) the profit and loss forecast is restricted to regular income items such as sales revenue and to running expenses.

If you are not confident about the format of a profit and loss account, turn to page 72 for a reminder.

You will find that the 'business starter packs' that you can get from the banks often set up a template for a monthly profit and loss account forecast, with comparative columns for estimated figures and also actual figures when they are known (see next page). This is a typical budget format; in fact the profit and loss account forecast is sometimes known as the 'operating budget'. For the purposes of your assessment, however, we recommend that you produce a profit and loss account forecast for the period of a year.

A typical bank 'proforma' profit and loss account forecast and a conventional profit and loss forecast produced by a business are compared on the next two pages.

# profit forecast

| | | month 1 | | month 2 | | month 3 | |
|---|---|---|---|---|---|---|---|
| | | budget | actual | budget | actual | budget | actual |
| **SALES INCOME** | | | | | | | |
| cash sales | | | | | | | |
| credit sales | | | | | | | |
| **TOTAL SALES INCOME** | A | | | | | | |
| | | | | | | | |
| **DIRECT COSTS** | | | | | | | |
| stock/raw materials | | | | | | | |
| sales commission | | | | | | | |
| other direct costs | | | | | | | |
| **TOTAL DIRECT COSTS** | B | | | | | | |
| | | | | | | | |
| **GROSS PROFIT** (A-B) | C | | | | | | |
| | | | | | | | |
| **VARIABLE COSTS/OVERHEADS** | | | | | | | |
| wages and salaries | | | | | | | |
| rent | | | | | | | |
| rates | | | | | | | |
| insurance | | | | | | | |
| heat/power | | | | | | | |
| telephone | | | | | | | |
| vehicle expenses | | | | | | | |
| stationery | | | | | | | |
| postages | | | | | | | |
| marketing/advertising | | | | | | | |
| travel | | | | | | | |
| bank charges | | | | | | | |
| interest and bank charges | | | | | | | |
| depreciation | | | | | | | |
| **TOTAL VARIABLE COSTS** | D | | | | | | |
| | | | | | | | |
| **NET PROFIT** | (C-D) | | | | | | |

This form would be extended to show budgeted figures (and actual figures when available) for a twelve month period. →

The figures from this forecast would in practice be summarised in the projection for the whole year shown on the next page. →

# FINANCIAL DATA – PROJECTED YEAR-END PROFIT STATEMENT

|  | £ | £ |
|---|---|---|
| Sales | | 480,000 |
| Purchases | 288,000 | |
| Less closing stock | 10,000 | |
| Cost of Goods Sold | | 278,000 |
| Gross Profit | | 202,000 |
| | | |
| Wages | 43,750 | |
| Directors salaries | 48,000 | |
| Rates | 2,900 | |
| Insurance | 1,500 | |
| Services | 2,400 | |
| Telephone | 1,200 | |
| Vehicle expenses | 2,400 | |
| Stationery | 600 | |
| Postages | 1,800 | |
| Marketing & advertising | 12,000 | |
| Office expenses | 6,000 | |
| Bank charges | 600 | |
| Interest | 7,500 | |
| Depreciation | 14,625 | |
| | | 145,275 |
| | | |
| Net profit | | 56,725 |

## evaluation of the financial plan - profitability

It is essential that a business should monitor its financial results when it starts trading so that it can evaluate the success of its planning. This is in part taken care of by the budgeting process. A business can also extract performance indicators on a regular basis. For example it can examine the periodic profit statements and balance sheets it draws up in order to calculate indicators such as gross and net profit percentages and return on capital employed. If the business has outside investors it will need to calculate investment ratios to reassure the investors that their money is providing a satisfactory return.

## projected opening balance sheet

The last essential document in the financial section of the Business Plan is the projected balance sheet of the business at the beginning of the first month of trading. Some business plans also include a projected balance sheet showing the position at the end of the year. The figures for the opening balance sheet will be available in the schedule of financial needs which is reproduced below. The numbers show where the figures in the balance sheet come from.

The only difference in figures is the working capital. The schedule below shows that the business can borrow up to £40,000 on overdraft to finance its day-to-day spending. When the business initially starts trading it has purchased stock for £24,000 (net of VAT) which is included as a current asset; this stock is financed by the overdraft for the same amount. As the business continues trading it will incur further costs during the month and so the overdraft will increase to cover this need.

## financial needs

| Item needed | £ | |
|---|---|---|
| office premises | 125,000 | 1 |
| computers | 45,000 | 2 |
| vehicle | 12,500 | 3 |
| office equipment | 12,500 | 4 |
| working capital | 40,000 | |
| TOTAL COST OF PROJECT | 235,000 | |

| to be provided by | £ | |
|---|---|---|
| own resources | 125,000 | 5 |
| bank finance: | | |
| commercial mortgage for office | 50,000 | 6 |
| business loan for computers | 20,000 | |
| overdraft for working capital | 40,000 | 7 |
| TOTAL OF FINANCING | 235,000 | |

## FINANCIAL DATA – PROJECTED START-UP BALANCE SHEET

|  | Cost £ | Dep'n £ | Net £ |
|---|---|---|---|
| **FIXED ASSETS** | | | |
| Premises | [1] 125,000 | 0 | 125,000 |
| Computers | [2] 45,000 | 0 | 45,000 |
| Vehicle | [3] 12,500 | 0 | 12,500 |
| Office equipment | [4] 12,500 | 0 | 12,500 |
|  | 195,000 | 0 | 195,000 |
| | | | |
| **CURRENT ASSETS** | | | |
| Stock | | 24,000 | |
| | | | |
| **CURRENT LIABILITIES** | | | |
| Overdraft | | [7] 24,000* | |
| | | | |
| **WORKING CAPITAL** | | | 0 |
| | | | 195,000 |
| | | | |
| **LONG-TERM LIABILITIES** | | | |
| Bank Loans | | [6] | 70,000 |
| | | | |
| **NET ASSETS** | | | 125,000 |
| | | | |
| | | | |
| **FINANCED BY** | | | |
| Authorised Share Capital | | | |
| 125,000 ordinary shares of £1 each | | 125,000 | |
| | | | |
| **ISSUED SHARE CAPITAL** | | | |
| 125,000 ordinary shares of £1 each, fully paid | | [5] | 125,000 |

**\*note**

Only £24,000 of the £40,000 overdraft was needed when trading started. It was required to pay for stock. The business still has a further £16,000 it can draw on to meet its future trading needs.

Remember that a balance sheet shows a 'snapshot' of the business on a particular day. In this case, on the following day the balance sheet will be probably be different – the bank account may change, stock may change, it may show amounts owed by customers (debtors).

## CHAPTER SUMMARY

- Finance for a business can be internal (such as personal savings) or external (such as bank loans and grants).

- Finance for business can be classified according to the time for which it is required:
  - short-term: 1 to 2 years
  - medium term: 3 to 10 years
  - long-term: 11 to 25 years

- When a business raises finance from a bank it will normally match the repayment period of the finance to the life of the asset, for example using an overdraft for working capital, and a ten year business loan for machinery, a commercial mortgage for premises.

- Financing is also provided from outside the banking sector: for example hire purchase and leasing from a finance house, venture capital from a merchant bank.

- The financial section of a business plan will contain a number of separate sections which explain how and why the business project is viable.

- A schedule of financial needs will summarise the sources of finance – where the money is coming from and how it will be spent.

- Budgets will estimate the amount of income that will be received from sales and also the money needed, both for start-up costs and also for running costs.

- A break-even calculation will work out at what level of sales the business will have covered its costs. The calculation can be carried out either by applying a formula, or by drawing a graph. The graph will provide more information for management than the simple calculation.

- A cash flow forecast will project the inflows and outflows of money through the bank account over a twelve month period. It is a useful forecast in that it highlights the months in which the business may need to borrow from the bank on overdraft. It also helps to prove the viability of the project.

- The profit and loss forecast (operating budget) projects profitability over a twelve month period. Like the cash flow forecast it helps to prove the viability of the project.

- The start-up balance sheet can largely be taken from the schedule of financial needs. It shows what the business is investing in and how the investment will be financed.

- The financial plan will need to be monitored on a regular basis by the extraction of performance ratios in order to evaluate the success of the plan.

## KEY TERMS

| | |
|---|---|
| **business loan** | normally a three to ten-year loan offered by the banks to finance purchase of assets such as equipment |
| **commercial mortgage** | a long-term loan – typically twenty five years – offered by the banks to finance the purchase of property |
| **overdraft** | short-term borrowing on a bank current account |
| **hire purchase (HP)** | an arrangement in which an asset is financed by a Finance House and will eventually pass into the ownership of the borrower |
| **leasing** | an arrangement in which an asset is financed by a Finance House but ownership of the asset normally remains with the Finance House |
| **factoring** | the purchase of the debts of a business by a specialist factoring company – it turns the working capital of the business into cash |
| **venture capital** | financing of a company by means of share purchase or loans by a specialist investment company |
| **Assisted Areas** | defined areas of the UK which are eligible for Government grants – Regional Selective Assistance |
| **variable costs** | costs which vary in line with the level of production |
| **fixed costs** | costs which a business will have to pay even if it does not produce any product |
| **break-even** | the point at which sales income equals running costs |
| **gross profit margin** | gross profit divided by sales and multiplied by 100 |
| **cash flow forecast** | a month-by-month projection of all the inflows and outflows of money through the bank account, normally over the period of a year |
| **profit and loss forecast** | a month-by-month projection of the profit of a business often with a summary projection of profit at the year-end; it is also known as an 'operating budget', containing comparative monthly columns for budgeted and actual income and expenses |

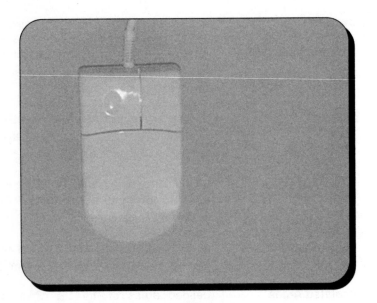

# www.osbornebooks.co.uk

Blank financial documents available for free
download from the Resources section

# index